# Exploring Poetry with Young Children

With the increased focus on children's language in Early Years education, poetry can be a valuable tool in enhancing speaking, listening and communication. This book provides parents and practitioners with a guide on how and where to start using poetry with children. Combined with practical suggestions on finding and using poems with children of differing ages and language abilities, it also offers advice on how to encourage children to create and develop their own poems.

*Exploring Poetry with Young Children* includes an anthology of a wide range of poems to use with children based on their everyday experiences, ensuring that adults can enhance the learning experience as it happens and enrich the language development of the children in their care.

Divided into two parts, this book covers:

- the nature of poetry and why it can be such an important part of our well-being;
- ways of using and sharing poetry with babies and toddlers;
- how to share poetry with children as they become confident users of language;
- the rhyming aspects of verse and ways in which these can be used to develop children's phonic awareness;
- the importance of establishing a poetic awareness in young children.

This will be an essential guide for all Early Years practitioners, students and parents who are interested in using poetry to develop the speaking, listening and communication skills of young children.

**Ann Watts** has worked as a nursery school head teacher, an Early Years adviser for Surrey County Council and then as an independent consultant. The main focus of this work has been leading training for Early Years staff as they develop their outdoor areas and consider how best to meet requirements of EYFS. She has also written a range of poetry for adults and for young children.

# Exploring Poetry with Young Children

## Sharing and creating poems in the early years

Ann Watts

Routledge
Taylor & Francis Group

LONDON AND NEW YORK

First published 2017
by Routledge
2 Park Square, Milton Park, Abingdon, Oxon OX14 4RN

and by Routledge
711 Third Avenue, New York, NY 10017

*Routledge is an imprint of the Taylor & Francis Group, an informa business*

*British Library Cataloguing in Publication Data*
A catalogue record for this book is available from the British Library

*Library of Congress Cataloging in Publication Data*
Names: Watts, Ann, author.
Title: Exploring poetry with young children : sharing and creating poems in the early years / Ann Watts.
Description: Abingdon, Oxon ; New York, NY : Routledge, 2016. | Includes index.
Identifiers: LCCN 2016003276| ISBN 9781138100497 (hardback) | ISBN 9781138100503 (pbk.) | ISBN 9781315657639 (ebook)
Subjects: LCSH: Language arts (Early childhood) | Poetry—Study and teaching (Early childhood)
Classification: LCC LB1139.5.L35 W343 2016 | DDC 372.6—dc23
LC record available at https://lccn.loc.gov/2016003276


ISBN: 978-1-138-10049-7 (hbk)
ISBN: 978-1-138-10050-3 (pbk)
ISBN: 978-1-315-65763-9 (ebk)

Typeset in Palatino
by Fish Books Ltd.

# Contents

# Figures

# Plates

# Acknowledgements

I would like to express my grateful thanks to the staff, parents and children from the following settings for welcoming me, sharing their ideas and giving permission to take the photographs for this book.

Crosfield Nursery School and Children's Centre
Peter Pan Preschool Nursery
St Christopher's School nursery class

Also to

Carol Gilbert for her wonderful black and white illustrations
Anne Addo for the poem 'Nursery days'
Joshua Grahame for his poem 'The crystal sea'

My extended family and four grandchildren, Joshua, Harry, Lucy and Wren who are now hearing more poems than ever.

Reggio Children Italy for permission to publish the poem 'The hundred languages' by Loris Malaguzzi, translated by Lella Gandini.

All poems in the anthology and Chapter 2 are written by the author unless otherwise acknowledged.

# Introduction

*Poetry makes you laugh, cry, prickle, be silent, makes your toenails twinkle. All that matters about poetry is the enjoyment of it however tragic it may be.*
*(Dylan Thomas 'A Few Words of a Kind' 1952)*

As adults, our experiences and enjoyment of poetry are often defined by our experience of poetry in childhood. In some schools poetry was "taught". It was analysed and reanalysed until the poem itself became lost in our minds. In other schools, children learnt poetry by heart and some schools offered poetry as an integral part of our literary heritage to be enjoyed and shared by all. Poetry is a way of using words to express our feelings at times of great emotion or simply to tell a story in a concise and memorable way. Poems can be used to tell stories, play games, sing songs, express feelings and describe scenes of beauty or tragedy.

The aim of this book is to inspire any adult who spends time with a baby, a toddler or young child to feel confident about using poetry to interact and share language and feelings. Poetry needs to be enjoyed together.

The book is written in particular for parents and practitioners who would like to share poetry with their children, but may be a little unsure of how and where to start. It offers an insight into the benefits of using poetry with children from a very early age. There are practical suggestions on finding and using poems with children of differing ages and language ability and advice on how to encourage children to create and develop their own poems.

The book includes a wide range of poems to use with children based on their everyday experiences. Having these to hand will ensure you can enhance the learning experience as it happens and enrich the language development of your children.

Chapter 1 discusses the nature of poetry and why it can be such an important part of our wellbeing as well as our literary heritage. It gives some definitions of poetry and explores why it is relevant in today's world

The second part of this chapter looks at the reasons for using poetry in the nursery. It explores the rationale for using poetry with very young children and the ways in which this can contribute to their development.

Chapter 2 focuses on using poetry with babies and toddlers. Singing traditional nursery rhymes is an important part of our literary heritage and there is a list of rhymes which are not used so often nowadays, but which many of us may remember from our own childhood. It looks at spoken verse and offers ideas for how to make up poems with babies and toddlers. It stresses the importance of rhythm, music and nursery rhyme in the development of listening skills. Using song and verse is a natural and instinctive way to soothe a baby and establishes a physical and emotional bond between adult and child. These bonds can be strengthened over time by continued use of suitable verse. There are suggestions of simple rhymes to use with babies. The use of finger rhymes and action rhymes is now recognised as an important factor in children's overall development.

The third chapter offers ways of sharing poetry with children as they become confident users of language. Poetry should be seen as an integral part of children's learning experiences rather than something separate. Having a rich repertoire of easily accessible poems enables adults to use a poem to support learning indoors and out. There are suggestions for planning indoor and outdoor spaces to enable children to have access to story and poetry books. Building poetry into the fabric of displays, parental newsletters and special homemade books are additional ways of ensuring poetry can be enjoyed by all. The chapter looks at the suitability of rhyming and non rhyming poems and gives examples of using poetry outdoors and also in forest school. There are also suggestions of additional resources to extend children's knowledge and enthusiasm for poetry.

Chapter 4 focuses on the rhyming aspects of verse and ways in which these can be used to develop children's phonic awareness linking in with aspects from *Letters and Sounds* (DfES 2007). It offers suggestions under the seven headings as given in Phase 1 Teaching Programme. Children who have grown up hearing rhymes and rhythms every day will enjoy being able to spot them for themselves and build up their knowledge to acquire skills of reading. Research has indicated that children who can recite eight nursery rhymes from memory become more fluent readers (Dunst, Meter and Hamby 2011).

In Chapter 5 there are suggestions to help adults to support children with creating their own poems. Case studies from different settings illustrate the importance of being able to let children have time to think and make their own suggestions. Encouraging children to think about the words they use will develop enquiring minds and exploratory attitudes. Children need to experience things for themselves and it is important that they have opportunities to find out about things, to be active learners and receive support from adults when they need it

The conclusion summarises the main points of the book and reiterates the importance of establishing a poetic awareness in our youngest children. By sharing poems with children we will also find that our own knowledge and love of poetry increases and hopefully adds an extra dimension to our lives.

The second part of the book consists of an anthology of poems written specifically for children in the Early Years Foundation Stage. The poems relate to the everyday experiences of young children. There are suggestions written in italics for different ways to use some of the poems. A wide selection includes poems on the seasons, the weather, growing things in the garden, pets, nature and wildlife, and going out in the big wide world. There are poems to use at times of celebration, poems to help with rhyme and rhythm and to develop an understanding of colours.

An internet search on poetry for early years reveals the need for practitioners to have suitable poems for use with our younger children.

*'Does anyone know any nice harvest/autumn poems or a good poetry book?'*

*'We are going to be doing a week's work on winter poetry focusing on using our senses. I've found it tough to find examples of any poems that fit the bill.'*

*'I'm looking for some simple rhyming poems on the theme of snow ice and the cold. I've had a good search on the net and haven't found what I'm looking for.'*

These are just some of the messages appearing in an educational forum.

This book of poems suitable for young children will enable adults to have an easily accessible resource and will also encourage children to share books with adults rather than rely on internet resources.

Poetry is an oral tradition which is centuries old. As you read poems to children you will be continuing this tradition. Unlike stories, poems are written specifically to be read aloud and reading aloud to children is an essential part of their language experience. Building a poem or rhyme into every story session will help children to become aware of poetic structures. Often at the end of a group story time there are a few spare moments and instead of reverting to a familiar nursery rhyme choose a poem which relates to something the children may have just experienced thus translating into expression what is still in the memory. Parents need to be encouraged to share books at bedtime and very often this may include a short poem or verse.

When you first open this book, find a poem that appeals to you. Try reading it out aloud on your own. Read it slowly and discover where to pause, where to use different tones and volume. Poetry should evoke an emotional response. If you enjoy a poem you will convey this sense of enjoyment to the children. These poems should be a starting point and enable you to become a confident user of poetry with children. As the poems relate so closely to the children's own experience, children will be able to understand, to enjoy and to absorb them. They will develop an awareness of sound patterns and words. This will help them with their own skills of reading but as they become more fluent users of language it is important to continue to offer them poems from other poets. There are suggestions to support this in the resource lists at the end of the chapters.

Nursery rhymes and finger rhymes for young babies, action songs and counting rhymes, poems about nature and the world we live in should all be part of the rich language experience we provide for children. It will not only give them a head start with their speaking and listening skills but it should be a time when adults and children enjoy language together and have fun.

## References

Department for Education and Skills (DfES) (2007) *Letters and Sounds: Principles and Practice of High Quality Phonics.* London: DfES.

Dunst, C. J., Meter, D. and Hamby, D. W. (2011) Review in *Centre for Early Literacy Learning* (CELL) Vol. 4, No 1.

Thomas, D. (1952) 'A Few Words of a Kind', a poetic discussion given at Massachusetts Institute of Technology on March 7. A transcription can be found on the internet at https://jasonkirin.wordpress.com/2013/10/16/dylan-thomas-a-few-words-of-a-kind/

# What is poetry and why do we need it?

This opening chapter considers the way in which poetry has been part of our lifestyle and heritage through the ages. It is important therefore that we do not neglect this important part of our literary heritage in our planning for children's learning. Even before birth babies become aware of sound patterns of music and speech and it is vital that we stimulate them from their earliest days by sharing lullabies, songs, rhymes and poetry. The chapter quotes the three prime areas of learning and the four specific areas of learning for the Early Years Foundation Stage and illustrates how poetry can be an integral part of these learning experiences.

## What is poetry?

Poetry existed in its earliest form before writing and scholars believe that using rhyme and repetition made it easier to remember the long stories that were told orally in order to preserve laws, history and genealogy. Many of the earliest known surviving poems are prayers or stories with religious themes, as well as some love songs and fiction. Poetry is often linked with music and again some of the earliest known poetry exists in the form of hymns.

If you type 'What is poetry?" into an internet search engine you will get many responses. The overriding response, however, seems to be that it is the use of imaginative language to express ideas and feelings. The word originates from the Greek word 'poema'. The literal translation of that word meant something that is made or 'created'. A very technical definition is given on Wikipedia:

> Poetry uses forms and conventions to suggest differential interpretation to words, or to evoke emotive responses. Devices such as assonance, alliteration, onomatopoeia and rhythm are sometimes used to achieve musical or incantatory effects. The use of ambiguity, symbolism, irony and other stylistic elements of poetic diction often leaves a poem open to multiple interpretations.

A more memorable definition however is a well known one from the poet, William Wordsworth, who described it as 'the spontaneous overflow of powerful feelings'.

For me, a poem is a juxtaposition of words and ideas so closely aligned that ideas give new meanings to words and words give new meanings to ideas. Poetry often demands an emotional and a visual response from the listener. Mind pictures are formed and there is a strong creative element in writing a poem.

Centuries ago, poetry was not regarded as a separate entity, but an integral part of oral culture and as such was combined with music, dance art and story. Our traditional nursery rhymes are an illustration of the way in which visual and musical interpretations have been handed down in verse form through generations. Most of the poetry that we are familiar with today, has been written during the last two centuries apart from, maybe, the sonnets and lyric poems of the sixteenth century.

Our modern culture, however, is beginning to recognise once more the importance of poetry and its impact on our daily lives. The origin of the post of Poet Laureate dates back to 1616. It is a royal appointment and very often, although there are no specific duties, the current laureate will write poems to celebrate occasions of national importance. There is now also a Children's Poet Laureate, thus demonstrating the importance of sharing and creating poetry for children.

## National Poetry Day

There is a national poetry day usually in early October when poetry takes over our air waves and is given a high profile in our towns and cities. Schools are invited to celebrate this too. It is organised by the Forward Arts Foundation and details can be found on their website www.forwardartsfoundation.org/national-poetry-day

National Poetry Day was founded in 1994 by William Sieghart who wanted to promote the work of poets and encourage people to read poetry as part of their everyday lives. There is usually a theme and the website publishes poems on the theme, but very often these are for older children. It is often possible to find something more suitable for younger children on the same theme, or if not why not focus on something that is happening in your setting and just share or create some poems about that.

Sir Andrew Motion set up a project in October 2015 as part of National Poetry Day to find out what poems remain in our memories. He said,

> Our pleasure in poetry is as natural as breathing, it forms a part of our foundation as individuals and the poems we commit to memory stay with us forever and grow as we grow.

There are now many more poetry competitions, one of the most recent being a competition to write a poem inspired by music heard at the proms concerts this year. In West Yorkshire poetry has been inscribed on the landscape. On the Pennine way there are seven poems written by Simon Armitage, on the theme of water and inscribed on the rocks. The website www.stanzastones.co.uk gives details of these and also gives guidance for family walks to each stone. There is a poetry seat carved out of rock, where it is hoped people may sit and create their own poems.

Until October 2014, Morag Styles was Professor of Children's Poetry at Cambridge University. She writes in an online article, 'The case for children's poetry',

> Poetry is an intense form of language. It can be simultaneously personal and universal it enlarges sympathies, helps us understand ourselves better, offers us insights about being human beings, it provides a way of working out feelings and giving order to experience by reducing it to manageable proportions.

People will write a poem when emotions are too powerful to be expressed in any other form, maybe at a time of birth or death or life threatening illness. Occasionally we are touched by a scene of particular beauty or an intricate detail in the natural world and this too can only be expressed in poem.

Whether or not the poem is heard by a large audience, shared with a few or kept a secret, is not important. The fact is that the writer has formed a poem as a vehicle for his feelings and emotions, sometimes voicing his innermost thoughts. Poetry helps us to be in tune with ourselves and if children are introduced to it at a young age they will hold onto it for life.

## Styles of poetry

Poetry for young children can be rhyming or non rhyming but should always contain rich language. It will often be a way of extending imaginary experiences and making them accessible. By encouraging children to recognise poetry as an art form in its own right, we will be offering something which hopefully will remain with them.

Poetry has a wide range of form and style – it could be a child's nursery rhyme, a nonsense verse, a limerick or a haiku. Early poetry took the form of long epic tales such as the Iliad or Odyssey. Some of the best children's stories of today use rhyming structures and are rather like the long epic poems of the Greeks. The story of 'The Gruffalo' is a tale of courage and wit as well as containing elements of danger. This is followed by 'The Gruffalo's Child' which uses the same form and epic structure.

Nowadays, there is much more poetry being written for children from the age of five upwards. Much of this is humorous and this in itself will make poetry a popular literary form for children to enjoy. Michael Rosen, Pie Corbett and Spike Milligan have all published books of poetry for older children. There is however, a growing realisation that children can enjoy poetry from a much younger age. In the introduction to *Poems for the Very Young*, Michael Rosen says that poetry is a particularly appropriate kind of literature to give to children.

Free form poetry is the term given to poems that do not rhyme. These poems may sometimes have an internal rhyme. Very often words are used that convey a sense of the sounds – onomatopoeia – or they may contain similar sounding letters. This is called alliteration and is a common feature of many poems. A considered and careful choice of words will often convey alliteration and a sense of rhythm can pervade the poem. Words that do not normally belong together will suddenly become meaningful and may suggest new ideas, simply by reason of where they have been placed in the text. However, there is not so much being written for very young children and this book seeks to explore the existing repertoire and make suggestions for how we can best share this with all children in the early years.

Poetry needs to be read aloud. Nowhere is this more important than in the nursery. Practitioners may need to read a poem aloud before sharing it with children. This familiarity will help them to read it with meaning and engage their young audience. Babies respond to rhythm patterns and rhymes from a very early age without necessarily understanding the meaning of the words. They are tuning in to the sound patterns and developing skills in listening and concentration. As they get older, they understand the meaning of the words and as their vocabulary increases they are able to explore non rhyming poems. Their own first attempts at writing poetry will usually be strings of non rhyming words. It is for this reason that this book contains rhyming and non rhyming poems

## Why do we need poetry in the nursery or in the home?

There is no simple answer to this question. If we examine the language environments of our young children we discover that poetry exists without any conscious effort on our part. As we rock a tiny baby, maybe sing a lullaby or a nursery rhyme we are using poetry. For centuries children have shared poems, music and stories through the oral tradition of reciting poems, telling stories, acting out plays and singing hymns and folk tunes.

Children from different cultures are still exposed to the poems and rhymes that their parents and grandparents have learnt and passed on. This tradition I am sure will continue but there is a need to consciously extend this into all aspects of children's lives through their formative years. Poetry should be an integral part of the collaborative learning experiences we offer to our children.

## Poetry as part of learning experience

Margaret Perkins, writing in *Bringing Poetry Alive* (Lockwood 2011, p. 27), cites a quotation from Ofsted in 2007, when they regarded an overemphasis on poetry just as a teaching tool as diminishing the actual power of poetry. They felt that poetry should be 'a medium for exploring experience rather than a teaching tool for language development'.

She states, that in her opinion too, the main aim of poetry with young children is to give them those imaginary experiences and the means through which they can express them and explore them further. In Chapter 3, there are suggestions for using poems to support children's learning as they engage in the Foundation Stage curriculum.

In the Foundation Stage curriculum there are now three prime areas of learning: Communication and language development; Physical development; Personal social and emotional development. This is then followed by four specific areas: Literacy; Mathematics; Understanding the world; Expressive arts and design.

If parents and practitioners become confident readers of poetry themselves and begin to share poems with their children, they will be able to offer a range of experiences which can support and extend learning in all these areas.

## Prime areas of learning

### Communication and language development

In the practice guidance for EYFS 2007 the early learning goal (ELG) for listening was 'listen with enjoyment and respond to stories, songs and other music rhymes and poems and make up their own stories, songs, rhymes, poems'.

In the revised version of EYFS 2014, this has been diluted to 'listen to stories accurately anticipating key events and respond to what they hear with relevant comments, questions or actions'. The fact that poems and rhymes are not specifically mentioned does nothing whatsoever to promote the cause of sharing poetry with our youngest children. There is, however, a requirement in Para 1.5 of the statutory framework to 'give children opportunities to experience a rich language environment'. By offering poetry as part of the everyday learning experiences for children, whether at home or in a nursery, we can enrich not only their language, but hopefully their lives as it becomes an integral part of their being.

When we visit a foreign country, we may not understand any of the language, but after a short time we become attuned to the sounds, the tones and the rhythms of the language. Poetry provides short sharp bursts of language where these same features are emphasised and even though babies and toddlers do not necessarily understand the meaning, they are becoming attuned to the sounds of the language being used. By six weeks old a baby is tuning into the sounds of the language it hears most and will lose the capacity to make other sounds specific to other languages. These are the first steps in speaking and listening. Children's attention span can be increased by the use of music or rhyme. A steady beat will engage very young children and children who are learning English as an additional language will find it easier to remember the words of a rhyme than a sentence.

Because poems defy the rules, they can often be easily understood – there are fewer words. Pupils who have limited English may find they can express something through a poem simply because they can forget about structures and use the vocabulary they have. They too will have been exposed to the rhymes and rhythms of their own culture from babyhood and rhythmic patterns when heard in English will offer a sense of familiarity and security.

A poem will often use new vocabulary and when children are invited to discuss their ideas or thoughts about a poem they will develop their own confidence and ideas. This is a skill which is highlighted in the Characteristics of Effective Learning (revised EYFS 2012). Details of this can be found on pages 4-5 of Development Matters, available online: www.foundationyears.org . Under the heading 'Creating and Thinking Critically' children should make links and have their own ideas. A poem seems a natural way for them to do this. The case studies in Chapter 5 illustrate clearly the richness of the children's own ideas.

## Physical development

Children should have opportunities to be active and interactive and to develop their coordination, control and movement. As we play with babies, we use physical contact – we lift them up, swing them or tickle them. Fun and enjoyment are established and when we use simple finger rhymes with toddlers we are continuing this experience.

Action rhymes and action songs are one of the earliest ways we introduce children to a steady rhythmic beat. Moving to a steady beat has been shown to be developmentally important in the processes of learning to read and write.

Children can re-enact their own experiences of splashing in puddles, planting and digging in the garden, as they join in with some of the rhymes and poems suggested later in this book. Chapter 2 discusses in more detail the importance of using action songs and rhymes with babies and young children.

## Personal social and emotional development

As we use poetry with our babies we are offering emotional support. Holding and rocking evokes the continuation of the rhythm of the heart beat that the baby hears in the womb and often can be the only way to soothe a young baby. This establishment of rhythm is an essential part of our relationship with a baby and should continue right through the first five years.

As children become more fluent in language, we can extend this experience and use poems to express our emotional feelings or responses to a scene or situation. We can encourage children to think more deeply about things and look more closely at the world around them. A poem can enhance this and be an expression of something the child has experienced.

Children need to learn how to develop 'a positive sense of themselves and others, form positive relationships and develop respect for others: to develop social skills and learn how to manage their own feelings (DfE, EYFS 2014, para 1.5) Poetry can offer a way to open up difficult subjects, the death of a pet or a person, suffering and also profound joy and happiness. Poetry will help to build resilience in children.

Evidence indicates that success in life depends on how well we know our own emotional makeup; how well we manage our emotional responses and react to the emotional responses of others. Jane Adams (2008) writing about emotional

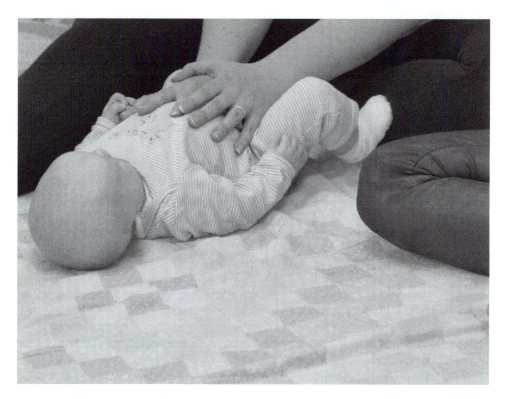

**FIGURE 1.1** Massaging your baby as you sing a rhyme or recite a verse in time with your movements can help their physical, emotional and language development.

intelligence suggests that 'People who have these skills are more likely to find success in the workplace and in their personal lives'.

Poetry seems to be a very natural and obvious way to help children to understand their own feelings and those of others. Two sections in Pie Corbett's, *A First Poetry Book*, offer easily accessible poems about 'Feelings' and 'Friends'. They acknowledge the feelings of jealousy, sadness or just being fed up and offer a way to deal with these that a young child can relate to and understand.

Elena Aguilar writing in an online blog for edutopia says:

> *William Butler Yeats said this about poetry: 'It is blood, imagination, intellect running together...It bids us to touch and taste and hear and see the world, and shrink from all that is of the brain only.' Our schools are places of too much 'brain only'; we must find ways to surface other ways of being, other modes of learning. And we must find ways to talk about the difficult and unexplainable things in life – death and suffering and even profound joy and transformation.*

## Specific areas of learning

### Literacy

Hearing poems on a regular basis can play an important part in children's literacy development. They will learn new and exciting vocabulary and the early years framework asks that children be given access to a wide ranging of reading materials, 'books, poems and other written materials'.

Unfortunately there is no emphasis on the importance of hearing poems – poetry is meant to be heard before children can read it for themselves. Sharing poetry with children can be a source of enjoyment for the adult as well as the child. Children learn to develop their listening skills and become more aware of the patterns of the words, letters and sounds that they hear.

The importance of using rhyme and rhythm to help children begin to link sounds and letters and begin to read and write cannot be stressed enough. More detail about this and ideas of how to work with children are given in Chapter 4.

### Mathematics

This area of learning involves 'providing children with opportunities to develop and improve their skills in counting, understanding and using number'.

Counting rhymes and simple finger rhymes provide an easily accessible way to encourage the development of understanding of number. Using fingers and toes is an instinctive way to count and subtract and if this can be accompanied by a memorable and enjoyable verse it is so much easier to retain the information. Young toddlers become familiar with the concept of two as they recite traditional verses. 'Two little dicky birds', 'Peter hammers with one hammer' and 'Tommy thumb' are well known nursery verses which reinforce the concept of two. Use the anthologies listed at the end of Chapter 3. The rhymes in the anthology in this book have been written in response to children either at home or in a nursery. Older children will enjoy counting rhymes and may well, with a little help, be encouraged to make up their own number poems. As children begin to understand and use numbers to five, introduce poems up to ten and so on. Some rhymes can be adapted to help children to understand number bonds of two e.g. *'Ten fat sausages frying in a pan, One went pop and the other went bang'* As children become more confident users of number bonds they may be able to use the same verse pattern to make up some counting rhymes with higher numbers.

### Understanding the world

Adults should, 'Guide children to make sense of their physical world and their community through opportunities to explore and observe and find out about people, places, technology and the environment'.

Poems have an important part to play in helping children make sense of the world they live in. Look through some of the poems in this book or in the listed anthologies. Poems about the seasons, the weather and some of the activities shared at nursery help children to revisit some of the experiences and may open up discussion or offer another perspective on something they have learnt. 'Autumn in the garden' is a good example of a poem where a child asks a question based on previous experience. The poem goes on to give an answer and an imaginative interpretation of new knowledge. The child is querying why they need to wear wellies when the sun is shining but the answer lies in the poem as it describes the autumn dew,

> Each leaf and blade is sparkling bright
> Dew comes down at dead of night
> Diamonds shining fresh and clean
> Dew drops on a bed of green

Hopefully this offers a more imaginative and appealing description than an adult just saying, 'oh it's the dew'.

There are several poems in the anthology section which describe outdoor experiences through using our five senses. There are poems which help children to understand the life cycles of plants and how we grow fruit, flowers and vegetables. There are poems which may increase children's knowledge and vocabulary with regard to the creatures they find and observe outdoors. Some poems in the listed anthologies give us moving insights into other cultures and life in other parts of the world. The poems should appeal to children and become a memorable way for them to gain understanding of these things.

## Expressive arts and design

The framework states adults should 'enable children to explore and play with a wide range of media and materials, as well as providing opportunities and encouragement for sharing their thoughts, ideas and feelings, through a variety of activities in art, music, dance role-play and design and technology'.

Chapter 5 suggests ways of helping children to use words to share their thoughts, ideas and feelings but to express them in a more creative form. Children are always very proud of their poems and will often enjoy illustrating them. An example of a project which combined art, movement, role play and design and technology is given in the case study of Peter Pan preschool (pages 69–71). Children heard and acted the story of the Minotaur. They built a maze with string and nails and made a model of the Minotaur. They created their poems about him, painted and drew pictures and moved like the Minotaur.

Poetry and rhyme is inextricably linked with music and dance. If children are singing, they are in all probability using a nursery rhyme or verse. It is through poetry that they can begin to enter the world of imagination. Roger McGough writing in the foreword to the *Macmillan Treasury of Nursery Rhymes and Poems*, describes how he had an exceedingly favoured childhood with access to a garden and a stream. This, however, was in his imagination as he lived in a back to back terrace,

**FIGURE 1.2** The children at Peter Pan Nursery move like the Minotaur as part of their creative project.

but it was through poetry that he came to find this world. His earliest memories were of listening to nursery rhymes and speaking them aloud with his mother.

As children become more competent users of language they may use poetry to express something that they cannot necessarily express through longer structures. Poetry can play an important role in developing children's imaginations and giving them a voice. There is a very moving example quoted by Michael Lockwood in his book *Bringing Poetry Alive* of an older child with special needs (p. 59) who states, 'People think I have no imagination but that's really where I live'.

The child composed a poem which is a vivid description of being locked in his own world, with trees and leaves for companions, and hearing the waves on a seashell, while life goes on all around.

## Conclusion

Jill Pirrie (1998) discovered that less able children have a natural affinity with writing poems and are able to write with a directness and simplicity of expression. It is important to offer poetry to all children, but we must begin with babies and ensure that we continue to offer this rich diet of inspired language as part of everyday learning whether at home or in a nursery setting. Parents and practitioners will discover as they revisit the poems of their childhood they will become more confident readers of poetry. Sharing poetry with young children can be an immensely satisfying and enjoyable experience. It can be a time for fun and laughter or it may be a time for calmness and quiet. It can be woven into every aspect of the early years curriculum and offers an imaginative approach to using language with our children.

## References

Adams, J. (2008) 'Developing emotional intelligence', *Child Care*, November.

Aguilar, E. www.edutopia.org/blogs

Department for Education (DfE) (2014) Statutory Framework for the Foundation Stage, available to download from www.gov.uk/government/publications: reference number DFE-00337-2014

Lockwood, M. (2011) *Bringing Poetry Alive*. London: Sage Publications.

Perkins, M. 'Teaching poetry in early years', in Lockwood 2011 see above.

Pirrie, J. (1998) *On Common Ground: A Programme for Teaching Poetry*, London: Hodder and Stoughton.

Styles, M. (2001) www.cam.ac.uk/research/discussion/the-case-for-children%E2%80%99s-poetry

www.foundationyears.org.uk/files/2012/03/Development-Matters-FINAL-PRINT-AMENDED.pdf

# Sharing poetry with babies and toddlers

*Children's responses to poetry are innate, instinctive and natural. Maybe it starts in the womb with the mother's heartbeat. Children are hard wired to musical language, taking pleasure in rhyme, rhythm and repetition and other patterns of language.*

*(Morag Styles 2011)*

This chapter focuses on the importance of using songs, poems and rhymes with babies from their very earliest days. There are examples of poems and lullabies that can be used with very young children and ideas for making up your own. The headings for the three prime areas of learning are used again as they emphasise the most important areas of development for children in the first two or three years of life.

Even before a baby is born, it develops an awareness of rhythm as it hears the heartbeat of its mother. There was an amazing video clip on Netmums in 2015 showing a prenatal scan taken at four months. As the parents sang the song, 'If you're happy and you know it', the tiny hands could be seen clapping in time. The doctor was so amazed they repeated the scan and the same thing happened again.

The first few weeks of life are dominated by the natural rhythms of sleeping, eating and crying as the baby struggles to come to terms with a new environment.

Anyone who has held a crying newborn will know how easily we slip into a steady rocking motion as we hold the tiny baby. In the next few months helping a child to settle to sleep will often involve rhythmic movement either on your shoulder or in a crib or pram. Very often, too, we may sing to soothe a child. Lullabies and nursery rhymes slip easily back into our memories and maybe it's just as well the baby doesn't understand the words as we sing about the cradle falling from the treetops. Music and rhythm are an essential part of the earliest weeks and months of life and we need to ensure that we can sustain this through the next few vital years. As I sang to my two week old granddaughter, I used the tune Frere Jacques with a variety of words. She was beginning to use her eyes and look around a little bit and as I sang she became transfixed and began to give eye contact and just held my gaze for several minutes as she listened.

Sally Goddard Blythe (2011) writes about the importance of singing lullabies and rhymes to children even before birth.

**FIGURE 2.1** This tiny baby is two weeks old and is focusing her gaze for the first time. She is fascinated when her grandmother sings to her and is also watching the movements of her tongue.

> *Lullabies act as a multisensory link for tiny babies between the womb and the new outside world. They are sung to soothe the baby but should also be used as a form of communication, as the sound of a parent's voice singing will stimulate the brain and encourage the development of listening skills which are so essential for language development. Lullabies share a similar range of rhythms which all seem to equate with the natural rocking and walking rhythms of adults.*

She cites the work of Michel Lazarev and the importance of both mother and father singing to their new born child. His work focuses in particular on the role of the father as the deeper voice range connects the child to a wider range of frequencies.

Babies use language to communicate from a very early age and will make different sounds to express different needs. A six month old can use a shout to attract attention rather than a cry and is beginning to move her body in time to a beat. As we play with babies, we need to use rhymes and rhythms in our daily interaction as well as maybe singing or rocking them to soothe them. Babies learn to listen as they grow inside the womb and they can distinguish a female voice from a male one and soon learn to recognise the voice of their mother. They are already tuning into sound patterns and by using rhythmic and repetitive language we are helping them to develop this skill. As we talk to very young babies it is interesting to note we often use questions, e.g. 'Are you the most beautiful baby in the world?' 'Are you going to give me a smile?' 'Who's a gorgeous boy?' etc.

As we use this form, our voice tone changes and there is an intonation which is slightly different from normal, everyday adult speech. Our voices go up at the end of the sentence and somehow this seems to sustain the baby's attention. It is as though we are instinctively using the type of speech which we would use when reading or reciting a poem.

Using poems and rhymes with tiny babies seems to be one of the very best ways to meet their needs in terms of the EYFS three prime areas of development: Communication and language, Physical and Personal social and emotional.

## Communication and language development

Shortly after birth, a baby is able to imitate and will move his lips to respond to an adult making lip movements. His brain is already beginning to respond and two way interaction like this is the beginning of communication. A baby will cry in different ways to indicate his differing needs. It is not long before the baby begins to make other sounds. Encourage these sounds by repeating them (if you can). Use the letter sounds in rhythm, repeating them or using words that contain those sounds. Putting your tongue to the front of your mouth and holding your face close to the baby will encourage these first lip and tongue movements which are so important for learning to talk. A baby who is only a few weeks old may respond by putting out his tongue in response to you doing the same thing.

Babies may begin vocalising anytime between the first few weeks and the second month, progressing from random experimental sighs and coos to sounds that are actually directed at people or objects. By six weeks to three months, most babies will have developed a personal repertoire of vowel sounds, cooing and gurgling.

Friedrich Froebel, one of the pioneers of early years education, realised the importance of singing to very young babies and wrote a set of 'mother songs'. These have been studied by Colwyn Trevarthen and he has gone on to compile a set of baby songs from different cultures. His work with babies also cites how parents described in a diary the enjoyment of their four month old daughter and the way in which she responded to nursery songs (2004).The songs often have four verses and four short phrases. There is often a rhyming pattern where the last syllable of the second line rhymes with the last syllable of the fourth line. Babies become able to predict the timing and the rhyming patterns of these verses and may begin to join in the singing, sometimes vocalising on the same word each time they hear the song. As children hear the same short rhymes and verses again and again, this will develop skills of listening and concentration as they begin to make sense of the sound patterns of their first language.

## Physical development

Physical development is encouraged firstly by a sense of security as the baby is held and rocked. As the baby grows stronger independent movements increase and this can be encouraged by touch and verbal encouragement and interaction.

Children need to spend time on the floor lying on their tummies and also on their backs. This helps them develop their own body awareness as they begin to kick and explore their hands and feet. Laying a baby on his back and then spending a few moments singing or reciting a rhyme will encourage eye contact, listening skills and concentration.

Rhymes which focus on different parts of the body encourage the beginnings of body awareness. These two simple poems should be said slowly as the adult gently uses the appropriate movements.

> Touch your shoulders
> Touch your knees
> Tickle your tummy
> Oh yes please
>
> Touch your ears
> And stroke your head
> Touch your cheeks
> It's time for bed

**FIGURE 2.2** Children need time on their backs and their tummies. This is encouraged in the baby group at Crosfield Nursery School and Children's Centre.

*This next jingle can be made more personal by using your first name or 'mummy', 'daddy' and the baby's name instead of 'my' and 'your'.*

> Touch your head
> Touch your nose
> Touch your fingers
> And touch your toes
>
> Touch my head
> Touch my nose
> Touch my fingers
> Touch my toes
>
> Tickle my head
> Tickle my nose
> Tickle your fingers
> Tickle your toes

Jane Williams writing in Chapter 4 of *The Genius of Natural Childhood* offers suggestions for poems to use as you massage your baby. She suggests that the adult uses a melodious voice not necessarily singing but emphasising the rhythm so the baby can physically feel the rhythm at the same time as hearing it.

## Personal social and emotional development

Our response to the growing baby continues to be an emotional and a physical one. We will hold a baby close or on our knees facing us and very often bounce it up and down and make up our own nonsense rhyme. Babies a few months old will respond to this by giving us a beaming smile or chuckle. Use simple nursery poems such as 'Pat a cake pat a cake', 'Round and round the garden', 'This little piggy went to market', etc. Having fun together is one of the best ways to strengthen the social and emotional bond between adult and child.

As you hold a baby use simple rhymes such as this one or just make up your own. The content is not as important as the sense of rhythm and repetition.

### Clap hands

*This simple rhyme was made up as I played with Lucy my granddaughter. Place the baby opposite you either propped up on a cushion or lying on the floor where you can lean over her. Use your own baby's name. Hold the baby's hands one in each of your hands and make the actions as you speak.*

Clap hands Lucy
Clap them high
Clap hands together
Reach for the sky

Clap hands Lucy
Clap them low
Clap hands together
Touch your toe

The physical connections that play such an important part in the emotional wellbeing of babies can be reinforced with simple rhymes using parts of the body. Babies and toddlers will soon respond to the fun of simple games and a sense of enjoyment of poetry will begin to develop from this early age. The vocabulary used also reinforces the language and vocabulary that children begin to learn.

**The body rhyme**

Clap your hands
Wriggle your toes
Shake your fingers
Rub your nose
Clap your hands
Stamp your feet
This is the way
To make some heat

Poems and rhymes can be used with toddlers that relate to their everyday experiences and it does not matter if they do not understand all the words. They will be tuning in to the different style of language as it is used in a poem.

Babies need to be taken outside and love to watch the patterns of moving leaves and hear birdsong. More complex rhymes such as these can be used to reflect this widening of experience

**Bounce baby bounce**

*If you can hold the baby above your head this is a good rhyme to use as you swing him up and down. Again it can be made more personal by using your first name instead of 'my' and the baby's name instead of 'baby'.*

Bounce baby bounce
Bounce up high
Bounce baby bounce
Look up to the sky

Bounce baby bounce
Reach up tall
Bounce baby bounce
Look up at the wall

Bounce baby bounce
On my knee
Bounce baby bounce
Look up at the tree

**Bubbles**

Bubbles bubbles every where
Floating gently in the air
Blow them low and blow them high
Rainbow colours in the sky
Drifting down to touch the ground
They gently burst without a sound

**Touching stones**

Hold out your hand with fingers so tiny
Feel the pebbles so cold and shiny
Feel the pebbles hard, smooth and round
Make a pile upon the ground
Stroke them, feel them, hold them tight
Roll them roll them left and right

## Enjoying finger rhymes with babies and toddlers

Simple finger rhymes are a wonderful way to engage small children. There is immediate physical contact, often a sense of fun and anticipation particularly if the rhyme involves a tickle or a shout. Use a finger rhyme whenever you can with a young baby. Sing or recite a poem during nappy changing, after a meal, and any time of day when the baby is alert and ready to play. Most adults will know a few rhymes and babies love to hear the same ones over and over again, but try to extend your repertoire or make up a few of your own as you play together. 'This little piggy went to market' and 'Round and round the garden' can be used with tiny babies. They don't need to be able to understand the meaning of the words but will soon learn to anticipate what is to come.

As part of her research for a Froebel Diploma, Jenny Spratt studied the way children responded to finger rhymes and soon came to realise that they have a more important role than is generally realised (cited in Bruce and Spratt 2011).

**FIGURE 2.3** Finger rhymes play an important part in children's development. This baby is already trying to copy the movements of his mother's fingers as she recites to him.

Babies' hand movements form a major part of their physical development. They are usually born with a palmar grip and this later develops into a pincer grip as they learn to hold and let go of objects. Finger rhymes help to coordinate hand and mouth movements and children will often begin to make the appropriate gestures before they can say the words. Understanding often comes before the actual ability to use words. Chapter 4 of the book *Essentials of Literacy* (2011), gives a fascinating and detailed account of Jenny's work and shows how finger rhymes can support the developmental process. She stresses however that finger rhymes are only part of the general culture of using rhyme with children and should be experienced as part of a rich curriculum which includes music, poems and stories.

Some well known finger rhymes to use are:

- 'Tommy thumb, Tommy thumb'
- 'Here is the beehive, where are the bees?'
- 'A little mouse lived in a hole'
- 'Five little peas in a pea pod pressed'
- 'Round and round the garden'.

## Enjoying music and poetry with babies and toddlers

Introducing music to children from an early age has been found to have a wide range of benefits. Music and poetry go hand in hand. Apart from listening to classical or contemporary music, most of the music we offer to babies and toddlers contains text in the form of a rhyme or song. Using instruments and small finger puppets is a valuable way of extending children's listening skills and words can be used alongside this. The National Literacy Trust is concerned that many children are entering school with inadequate communication skills, often because parents have not helped these to develop. One of the most effective ways to encourage this is for parents to sing to their children. According to Sally Goddard Blythe, a consultant in neuro-developmental education, parents should sing to their children every day to avoid language problems developing in later life. Too much emphasis in the early years is placed on reading, writing and numeracy, and not enough on the benefits of singing. She also claims that listening to, and singing along with rhymes and songs uses and develops both sides of the brain.

### Musical instruments

Hold the shaker
Hold it tight
Move it round
With all your might

Hold the shaker
Let it shake
What sort of sound
Can you make?
Shake shake shake shake shake

Hold the drum
Shiny and round
See if you
Can make a sound
BANG BANG BANG BANG BANG

## Enjoying traditional nursery rhymes

With the impact of global technology societies and cultures are becoming increasingly conscious of the importance of oral storytelling and tradition. Many of our English nursery rhymes may have their origins as far back as the Middle Ages and some of the rhymes were passed down orally until Victorian times, when they were written down and deemed suitable for using with young children in the nursery. By

**FIGURE 2.4** A young child enjoys using small finger puppets as she listens to songs and rhymes in a 'musical bumps' session at Crosfield.

using these rhymes with your children you will be continuing this tradition and grandparents, parents and children alike can derive the same enjoyment from using these rhymes.

The meanings of the rhymes may not be particularly appropriate for babies or children but that does not seem to matter. What is important is the sound of the words, the rhythms and the word patterns. Many have a strong and steady beat which can be emphasised as you recite or sing them.

Blythe (2011) reiterates that singing traditional lullabies and nursery rhymes to babies and infants before they learn to speak, is an essential precursor to later educational success and emotional wellbeing. Traditional songs aid a child's ability to think in words. 'Songs and rhymes of every culture carry the "signature" melodies and inflections of a mother tongue, preparing a child's ear, voice and brain for language'.

Michael Sizer has written an interesting online article on 'The surprising meanings and benefits of nursery rhymes' at www.pbs.org. He refers to the importance of continuing the oral traditions and gives four reasons to use them with children. They are 'good for the brain' helping to build memory skills and if used within a book reinforce the visual experience of book sharing. They provide a source of fun and enjoyment, are good for using with groups of children and they preserve a culture which spans generations. He concludes that the true value of a nursery rhyme is the joy of a child's discovery of an old, shared language.

Recent research has stated that if children can recite eight familiar nursery rhymes by the age of eight they will be better readers. The research does not give a clear idea as to why this might be but it should definitely encourage us to use a wider repertoire in the very early years of a child's life.

Findings reported in Dunst, C. J., Meter, D. and Hamby, D. W. (2011) explore the relationship between young children's nursery rhyme experiences and knowledge and phonological and print-related abilities.

> *Recent surveys (Booktrust, 2009), studies (e.g., Libenson, 2007), and both the educational (Scholastic Education PLUS, 2009) and popular (Syson, 2009) media report that fewer parents nowadays engage their children in nursery rhyme activities either because they do not consider them to have educational value or that they believe nursery rhymes are "old fashioned" or find them embarrassing to recite to their children. More disconcerting is the fact that only about 50% of the youngest generation of parents know all the words to traditional nursery rhymes (Booktrust, 2009). An important role early childhood practitioners can play as part of early literacy learning interventions for young children with disabilities is to promote parents' understanding of the importance of nursery rhymes for their children's emergent reading and writing competence.*
>
> *(Dunst, Meter and Hamby 2011)*

The government currently funds a scheme called Bookstart, where every newborn baby receives a gift of books. The first pack for babies contains two or three hard back books and a rhyme sheet. This sheet has the words of the most familiar nursery rhymes and should encourage parents to start using these with their baby. The Bookstart website gives useful links to local library sessions and has a series of illustrated rhyme times sheets which can be downloaded,

**FIGURE 2.5** The Bookstart scheme encourages parents to read poems and rhymes from the moment their baby is born. Here the parents are looking through the pack while grandma is singing one of the rhymes.

### Observation notes taken from 'Musical bumps' sessions with babies and toddlers at Crosfield Children's Centre.

As part of the family services at Crosfield, there are two music and rhyme sessions each week for parents and young children. One is for babies under a year and the other is for toddlers up to the age of three. The sessions are run by Marie who works for a company called Musical Bumps. She runs a well planned session and it is amazing how even young babies remain so focused for anything up to an hour. They have one to one interaction with their parents and it is wonderful seeing the responses of both the parent and the baby. Marie uses a wide range of nursery songs and rhymes. Sometimes she sings unaccompanied and sometimes she uses a CD. The accompaniment is sensitive and balanced. In 'The Grand old Duke of York' the musicians use mediaeval instruments to give a different sound.

At the beginning of the baby session, Marie sings a welcome song to each baby in turn using the baby's name. She tells the parents a little about why we should sing to babies and use rhymes with them and explains that it is important to place the baby where he/she can see the adult's face and this will enable better interaction.

She uses nursery rhymes and nursery verses in the session choosing ones with a strong beat. As she sings 'Humpty Dumpty' she encourages mums to hold the baby up and then let the baby slide down in their arms. Similarly with 'The grand old duke of York' babies are held up, down and halfway up to

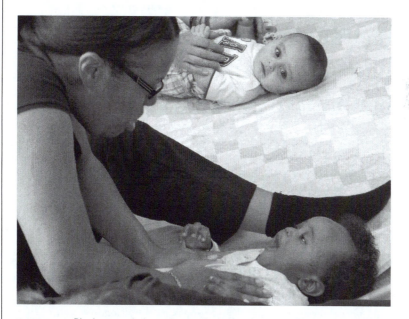

**FIGURE 2.6** Placing your baby so he can look directly at your face encourages better interaction.

match the words. The same song can be repeated using different speeds and volumes. Suitable instruments are given to the babies and they are encouraged to use them with music and then stop as the music stops. There is a time when parents move around holding babies on the shoulder and singing or listening to a rhythm which matches the walking speed. At the end of the session, babies are held and rocked to a nursery lullaby tune, so there is a gentle calm atmosphere and usually even fretful babies respond. There is a very strong feeling of emotional attachment between parents and children.

Using instruments with babies shows how they are listening and can respond. Stopping with the music can be difficult for older children but some of the babies responded and others were fascinated with the sounds they were making with the instrument. Over time however I felt they too would learn to control their responses. If you have young babies in your setting try it sometime!

In the toddler session, Marie uses a wide range of well known songs but will always try to introduce new ones. There is a CD available for parents to use at home with their children (see list of resources). Lots of action songs keep children's attention and they respond and join in well. Strong emphasis is put on sounds and rhythms and moving in time to the beat. Children also use instruments for some of the songs, as using a steady beat with children helps to develop physical coordination as well as listening skills.

These sessions showed how well very young children can focus and sustain listening when music and verse is used together. It was very obvious just how much the children were enjoying themselves and the mothers had quality time with their children but were also part of a larger group.

## Conclusion

As far as using rhyme, songs and poems with very young children, it seems to be that starting early and using a wide range enables us to offer children the best possible opportunities and experiences. Poetry contributes to the most important aspects of child development offering rich language experiences as well as physical and emotional interaction. Physical development is encouraged by clapping and moving in time to a steady beat.

Use every possible opportunity to share a rhyme with a baby or toddler and plan group times in nursery settings to offer rich experiences, maybe using instruments and a wide variety of music.

Many nursery settings, local libraries and children's centres offer group sessions for babies and toddlers. It is fascinating to observe ways in which even the youngest children respond to the rhymes and songs they hear. As they get slightly older they show a developing social awareness as they become aware of the other children in the group.

**FIGURE 2.7** Encourage parents to attend rhyme sessions and story times at their local library. This baby is enjoying hearing a musical instrument and focuses well on the group leaders.

## Useful additional resources to use with babies

Body rhymes: 'Heads, shoulders, knees and toes', 'Hokey cokey', 'One finger one thumb', 'This little piggy'.

Finger rhymes such as 'Round and round the garden', 'A little mouse lives in a hole', 'Five little peas in a pea pod pressed'.

*It's Time for Musical Bumps, Lullaby Baby, Up and About it's a Lovely Day.* These 3 CDs can be ordered from the website see www.musicalbumps.com. Click on 'Music for starters' and follow the shopping page. Or email info@musicalbumps.com

*This Little Puffin,* by Elisabeth Matterson Reissue 1991 Puffin.

*The Puffin Baby and Toddler Treasury,* 2008 Penguin a book for adults and very young children to share.

*Lift the Flap Animal Flap Book,* by Rod Campbell 1995 MacMillan Children's Books.

## Nursery rhymes

Use this alphabetical list to jog your memory. This will increase your repertoire and if you cannot remember the words, use one of the books listed below or try an internet search.

Baa baa black sheep
Bye baby bunting
Here we go round the mulberry bush
Hey diddle diddle
Hickory dickory dock
Hot cross buns
Humpty dumpty
Hush a bye baby
Hush little baby
I had a little nut tree
Jack and Jill
Jack Sprat
Jingle bells
Lavender's blue
Little Bo Peep
Little Jack Horner
Little Miss Muffet
London bridge is falling down
Lucy Locket
Mary Mary quite contrary
Mary had a little lamb
Old King Cole

Old MacDonald had a farm
Old Mother Hubbard
One, two, three, four, five
Oranges and lemons
Pat a cake
Polly put the kettle on
Pop goes the weasel
Pussy pussycat where have you been?
Ride a cock horse
Ring a ring of roses
Rock a bye baby
See saw Marjery Daw
Sing a song of sixpence
The big ship sails on the alley alley o
The grand old Duke of York
The North Wind doth blow
This is the way the ladies ride
Three blind mice
Three little kittens
Tom Tom the piper's son
Where oh where has my little dog gone?

The website www.rhymes.org.uk lists many more rhymes but also gives a history of many of our traditional rhymes and video clips of the most common ones.

Many nursery rhyme books are available with a CD. These can be used but it is important always to sing directly to children and support them as they join in and begin to use the words. Encourage them to develop their own voices to find a whispering voice and a singing voice. Children will this way learn that songs and poems use different voices.

*The Oxford Nursery Rhyme Book* Iona and Peter Opie OUP 1963.

*Usborne Illustrated book of Nursery Rhymes* edited by Felicity Brooks and Laura Rigo.

## References

Bruce, T. And Spratt, J. (2011) *Essentials of Literacy from 0-7*. London: Sage.

Dunst, C. J., Meter, D. and Hamby, D. W. (2011) Review in *Centre for Early Literacy Learning* (CELL), Vol. 4, No 1.

Goddard Blythe, S. (2011) *The Genius of Natural Childhood: Secrets of Thriving Children*. Gloucestershire: Hawthorn Press.

Styles, M. (2011) *The Case for Children's Poetry: A Discussion*, 11-10-2011 www.cam.ac.uk

Trevarthen, C. 2004 *Learning About Ourselves From Children: Why a Growing Human Brain Needs Interesting Companions.* University of Edinburgh.

www.pbs.org/parents/education/reading-language/reading-tips/the-surprising-meanings-and-benefits-of-nursery-rhymes/ article by Michael Sizer

www.bookstart.org.uk/about/packs/

www.bookstart.org.uk/usr/library/documents/rhymesheets/rhymesheet-sheets-2007.pdf

# Sharing poetry with young children

The main aim of this chapter is to encourage all adults, parents and practitioners alike, to share poems with young children on a daily basis. Poems should become an intrinsic part of a child's collaborative learning experience. There are suggestions for poems for parents to use at home as well as ideas for use in a group or nursery setting. The chapter suggests ways of including poetry in the literacy curriculum and also the physical environment of a nursery setting. There are suggestions too, for ways to use rhyming and non rhyming poems as children's understanding of language develops. Poetry can be used outdoors to support a wide variety of learning experiences. The anthology in this book and the resource lists at the end of this chapter offer a comprehensive collection of poems and in particular there are many about everyday experiences such as growing and planting, discovering the seasons or experiencing different kinds of weather. There is a short case study which shows how poetry and song can be used when outdoors and also the important contribution that poetry can make to the imaginative and creative development of children.

## Sharing poems with children from the age of two to five

If children hear poems on a regular basis they will become increasingly aware of the structures, form and poetic language. This in turn, will facilitate some of the activities described in the next two chapters. However, it must be stressed that poetry needs to be shared with children primarily for enjoyment. Reading or reciting appropriate poems aloud to children can be an immense source of satisfaction for both adults and children. A short poem will often engage children more readily than a story and they are able to concentrate for the entire length of a poem. By reading and becoming familiar with a poem yourself before sharing it with children, you will be able to read with expression and intonation. Gesture and emphasis all play an important part in poetry sharing. If you are familiar with the poem you will be able to offer eye contact with the children, again encouraging them to engage and participate. If you can memorise parts of it, this will also help you to give the children your full attention and add to the drama of the situation.

The previous chapter discusses the importance of using rhymes and poems with babies and toddlers. Children respond to rhymes from a very early age and as their vocabulary increases they will become responsive to poetry that is non rhyming, particularly if the poem is relevant and based on something they have experienced. A poem allows the growth of imagination. They will be able to listen to poems and see the colours of the poem, or imagine the sounds and sights that it evokes.

Poems need to be read to children as often as possible. There are often spare moments during the day, maybe at the end of a story session or waiting for parents to collect children. Practitioners may revert to singing a familiar nursery rhyme but perhaps this is the time when a new and less familiar rhyme could be introduced. It may be possible to find a poem which links to something that has happened during the session.

Try to plan poetry into your day and week. By becoming familiar with the anthologies you will be able to find poems that link in with the stories you plan to tell and with the activities that the children are doing. A poem of the week is often more beneficial than the old idea of a letter or colour of the week, as it should be relevant to other things the children are experiencing and hopefully will be appropriate for all children to enjoy.

## Raising staff awareness in a nursery setting

A short informal discussion between staff members will often be a good way to encourage a wider use of poetry. As in the case of Peter Pan nursery, (case study in Chapter 5), staff may not feel they use poetry very much, but on reflection and discussion, begin to realise that they are using more than they think. Rhyming stories are commonly told in most settings and these are a longer form of poetic verse rather like the original Greek epic tales. All settings will use a few of the basic nursery rhymes and songs but try to extend this and use new and less familiar ones. Good CDs are easily obtainable if you need help with tunes and the words of many poems can be found on the internet. There are some suggestions at the end of this chapter.

## Encouraging and involving parents

Questionnaires received from parents in one setting showed that many of them enjoyed using rhymes and songs with their children. None, however, were reading poems to their children on a regular basis. Try to encourage this and maybe have some books of poems available for them to borrow or suggest they try a local library. Many parents will have been involved in the Bookstart programme. Some of the books they were given may include poems and rhymes. One support teacher makes laminated cards of the Bookstart poems for toddlers and they can be used as pushchair books. This is one way to demonstrate to parents the importance of making rhymes and poems available. Even if children cannot read the words they begin to associate the book with the rhyme, they enjoy the pictures and often can recite some or all of the poem.

If children create their own poem, celebrate this by sharing it with the class group and other children in the setting. At Crosfield, the poem about the blossom (see case study in Chapter 5) was sent to parents in an attractive newsletter. This shows that the setting recognises the importance of poetry as part of children's learning experience. This message will hopefully encourage parents to share poems with their child.

The National Poetry Foundation has conducted some small research projects and in 2014 Dame Judi Dench revealed that she learns a new poem each day to keep her mind active. She said her love of poetry came from her father who used poetry almost as part of everyday speech and routines. Following on from this they discovered how parents can influence their children.

> In our previous research project, a much smaller study of local poetry teachers, we found that the teachers who knew some poetry by heart had all had a parent who recited poetry to them as children – and it was nearly always a father. Our sample was by no means large enough to make any claims about this, but evidence from other sources certainly supports the idea that poetry is transmitted in vivo. And the idea that it might tend to come down through fathers is a most intriguing one.
>
> (www.poetryandmemory.com)

Some parents may attend groups with their young babies as seen in the Crosfield case study in Chapter 2. Try to find time to talk to parents about the rhymes they have used with children and in particular encourage parents to give examples of poems and rhymes from their own culture. If you do not know a particular language ask parents if they could come in to read a few poems to a group of children. Children love hearing the sound of language whether it be their own or that of one of their peers. If you decide to have a 'poem of the week', share this with parents so they can use it at home with their children.

## Where can I find suitable poems?

Many adults now use internet searches for resources to use with children. There are many websites which offer poems related to a number of topics but there is a very varied approach and many of the rhymes there are simplistic and do not use particularly rich language. Finding resources online can be very time consuming and if adults are able to read poems to children from a book this will reinforce the message that books are still a valuable learning resource.

Finding suitable poems is not always easy but the anthology in this book includes poems that can be used throughout the year indoors and outside as part of children's learning experience. Many of the poems can be used to support the outdoor learning that is such an essential component of effective early years practice. There is a list at the end of this chapter of most of the available resources suitable for children in the Foundation Stage.

## Using poems at home

For parents, sharing poems with children can offer immense enjoyment. Using one of the illustrated anthologies such as the *Macmillan Treasury* (see resource list) provides shared, special time where the child can cuddle in and look through a book with an adult. The child will soon begin to ask for favourite poems time and time again. Children are initially attracted by the clear and colourful illustrations but as time goes on they learn to listen carefully to the rhythms and patterns of the language and then begin to make sense of the words.

Emotional and physical comfort is also an important part of this sharing experience and will play a part in fostering a lifelong love of books and poetry.

**FIGURE 3.1** Ollie and his mum enjoy looking at the *Macmillan Treasury of Rhymes and Poems* together.

## Using poems in a nursery setting

My own interest in sharing poems with young children began with the original edition of *This Little Puffin* by Elisabeth Matterson. It was invaluable and as I began to appreciate how well young children responded to the poems I used, I began to write a few poems of my own to fit in with the children's learning experiences. This has inspired more writing and many of the poems in this book have been written to support learning experiences of children at home and in nursery settings. A revised edition of *This Little Puffin* is now available and this is well worth buying. It contains a wide variety of poems, rhymes, songs and games with guidance on using finger rhymes and music for some of the songs. Another one which should be in every nursery setting is *A First Poetry Book* edited by Pie Corbett and Gaby Morgan. The sections on nature, seaside, friends and minibeasts contain many poems that can be used with children around the age of three. By dipping into this book you will find many poems that you will enjoy using with your children. There are poems too about feelings, written in a way that children can understand and relate to as they struggle with their own emotions.

## Creating a rich language environment in your setting

It is vital that children are able to respond to the languages spoken around them. Many children now grow up in homes where more than one language is used on a daily basis. Children have an amazing capacity to absorb languages and it is important that we offer language rich environments in our homes and nurseries.

The most important language resource for children is the adult who spends time listening to them, sharing their conversations and extending their thinking. We know the importance of asking open-ended questions and giving children time to think of their own responses. As you read a poem with your children, ask them if it reminds them of anything or whether there are any parts of the poem they particularly like or dislike. At Crosfield one member of staff enjoys poetry and was asked to work with a small group of able children. Although this was early in the school year and the children were only three, she brought into school her own copy of *100 Best Poems for Children* (see resource list) and wanted to share some of them with the children. She used a range of poems and as she said 'the children might not understand all the words and meanings but I just want them to hear the sounds and rhythms of the language'. They heard a poem about Halloween and one child noticed an illustration of leaves falling from a tree 'Autumn, that's autumn', he said. The discussion then moved onto what happens in autumn. They listened to one of the poems in the anthology in this book and were asked about the words 'ruby' and 'gold'. They did not know what ruby was but one child said, "gold: gold coins it's like treasure; the trees have treasure'. Children went outside to look at some of the leaves more closely. They looked at the colours and made up a short poem.

> *Yellow green orange brown see the leaves come falling down.*

This was printed out for them to look at and illustrate if they wished. Leaf play outdoors followed this session and leaves were used in many different ways by groups of children as well as children playing on their own. The poem had instigated and encouraged leaf play.

In addition to interacting with children's conversations, adults are also responsible for creating an environment which offers maximum opportunity for children to use and hear language. Words and text need to be built into the spaces and it is advisable to give as much time to the initial layout of indoor and outdoor space as possible. Reflective practice will allow adults to respond and make changes to reflect the children's learning needs.

## Using poetry in displays

Make displays in the nursery as interactive as possible. This gives children additional opportunities for spontaneous and imaginative play and will often stimulate conversation between children and also between children and adults. Use any vertical spaces for pictures and photographs but try to include a poem as well. Use a small horizontal space with as many displays as possible and provide small world figures or appropriate artefacts for children to handle and move around. This will stimulate discussion and often imaginative play.

### Story displays

If the display is based on a popular story, use a small table or the top of a unit beneath the display to provide some figures and props from the story. The children will enact out their own versions and may offer different interpretations. *Owl Babies* is popular and some fluffy toy owls, a branch and some moss and twigs can be provided. It is now possible to buy models based on the actual illustrations from the book. Story bags and story sacks too can be used in conjunction with displays. Displays often contain some text, maybe a caption or some sound words that are relevant. Think of a short poem that fits in with the subject of your display, type it out and place it on the wall. This will enable any visitors, parents or staff members to be able to share a relevant poem with children. For example, the finger rhyme, 'There's a wide eyed owl' found on page 240 of *This Little Puffin* would fit in well with the *Owl Babies* display.

### Seasonal displays

Many settings create displays that reflect the current season. It is important to emphasise here that children need to be taken outside and experience the changing colours, the temperature and changing light for themselves. They need support to help them develop an awareness of the patterns of growth during our year but an indoor display can often create a focal point where children discuss their own experiences. There may be pictures of the children themselves engaging in a seasonal activity e.g. planting seeds or bulbs. There may be collections of natural objects. Sometimes there are seasonal flowers and fruits. Try to include a short poem in the display. If this is used with a group of children at story time and then pointed out to them within the display, children will soon begin to develop an awareness of poetry as being part of the their whole learning experience not something that happens in isolation.

## Festival displays

Again using the principles above, try to include poems written by the children or by an adult to reflect the theme. In a display about Chinese New Year there was a printed poem on the wall and the children used this as a basis for their art work.

Bonfire night often features on the walls of nursery settings. Children are encouraged to use a range of art materials to recreate some of their experiences of fireworks. Again why not include a bonfire poem? Use one of the bonfire night poems at the back of this book to go up on the wall with the children's firework paintings or photographs of fireworks.

Screaming rockets
Exploding so bright
Coloured stars shining
Amidst the dark night

Catherine wheels spin
An explosion of light
Fiery gold circles
A wonderful sight

Sparklers twinkle
As we wave them around
I like them best
They don't make a sound

**FIGURE 3.2** A bonfire poem from the anthology is used in this display about fireworks.

## Colour displays

Many settings often still have a colour themed display to encourage colour recognition. This can however be taken much further and used to stimulate language and conversation. It is important to include objects that are intrinsically the right colour – very often objects from the natural world fall into this category. A red plastic bucket and spade is not as essentially red as a shiny red pepper. A spray of autumn leaves, scarlet and crimson may be set against a photograph of a red squirrel or a sunset streaked sky. A poem from the colour section in the anthology could be printed out using coloured ink and maybe illustrated by the children for the display. Use children's own work too and encourage them to learn a short colour poem.

## Planning the physical space indoors and out

It is important to think about the physical environment and create places where children can talk to each other or where they can sit quietly with a book. Look at small corners, or try to think of ways to divide larger spaces either with screens or low furniture. Outside it may be possible to plant some fast growing shrubs or trees to create small enclosed spaces. This in turn can attract a variety of insects and small creatures which will often provoke discussion and conversations. Poetry needs to be integrated into the whole literacy experience you are offering your children.

This willow cabin is attractive but can be expensive. If you have a large bush you may be able to create a den inside it by carefully pruning out some inner branches. A rug and a cushion and maybe a homemade rhyme book or story book can create a magical space for children to enjoy looking at books.

Outdoor and indoor spaces can be made attractive by using fabrics and appropriate seating. Small logs or cushions mean that children are comfortable and can engage in conversation with each other. Picnic rugs and cushions are an easy way to give the message that it is fine to use the outdoor space to sometimes sit quietly. This will also offer opportunities for children to observe what is going on around them and if an adult can sit with them, interesting discussions may follow concerning the small creatures, the scents, sights and the sounds of the garden.

Books of all kinds should be readily available both indoors and out. Story books, nonfiction reference books and poetry books should be provided. If there are poetry books nearby, it may often be possible for the adult to choose a suitable poem and

**FIGURE 3.3** A den or willow cabin makes a pleasant place to sit with a book. Encourage the use of poetry books and rhymes outside.

read it aloud to the children. This could happen spontaneously, as the occasion demands or it may be that the adult could use a poem to reinforce the active learning that has taken place. This is a good way of extending children's literacy but also supporting previous learning. A poem will often provoke some discussion and new ideas may follow. Children may be encouraged to revisit their experience after hearing a poem about it and develop their interactions or thought processes.

## A listening corner

Many settings have a space where children can use their own tape recorders or CDs to listen to music or stories. If you are able to create a small space and have some tape recorders try to tape some of the children's favourite poems. Make different versions of the same poem using different voices: both adults' and children's. Parents may be able to help with this and you could build up a supply of poems in different languages and from different cultures.

## Book or story corner

Look at the way books are arranged in your book area. If possible have a bookshelf, a basket or an attractive box just for poems. Nursery rhyme books can be kept here too. Encourage children to recognise which books should be kept here. Try to work with your parents and encourage them to provide rhymes, songs and poems in their own languages. A rough translation might be useful for staff members not familiar with a particular language.

Include a book of number and counting rhymes in your poetry box or on the poetry shelf. There are many familiar number rhymes and there are some included in this book. Have a go at making up your own with the children. Just seeing their attempts in print alongside perhaps some drawing or clip art illustrations will inspire confidence as well as develop their numeracy skills. There is an example of this in the next paragraph.

## Counting rhymes

Counting rhymes should be used regularly as they help children begin to understand the conservation of number and the basics of addition and subtraction. Some traditional nursery rhymes can be used too and the following ones support children's growing understanding of number concepts. 'One two three four five, once I caught a fish alive' and 'One two buckle my shoe' both use the one to ten sequence of numbers.

There are many well known counting rhymes. 'Five currant buns in bakers shop', 'Five speckled frogs' and Five little ducks' all feature regularly in many settings.

Composing a simple counting rhyme is not too difficult and could be done with a group of children to support the learning experiences at the time. Some examples of poems created and used in the classroom to support children's learning are 'Five yellow daffodils', page 93 and 'Five little fireworks', page 158.

The rhyme 'Ten red tulips', page 126 could be used with children with greater understanding of numbers up to ten.

If you can create a rhyme with your children write it out, maybe illustrate and laminate it for them to look at. You may be able to make a small collection in a book for children to handle and read amongst themselves.

The following poem was written at home for my grandson's fifth birthday to help him to understand numbers to five. It was printed out on a laminated card for him to keep. We had turkey dinosaurs for tea!

5   Five turkey dinosaurs were making such a roar
    Harry came and ate one and that made four
4   Four turkey dinosaurs were stomping past a tree
    Joshua came and ate one and that made three
3   Three turkey dinosaurs wondering what to do
    Lucy came and ate one and that made two
2   Two turkey dinosaurs were playing in the sun
    Mummy came and ate one and that made one
1   One turkey dinosaur was sitting by a stone
    Grandpa came and ate him and that made none

I would hesitate to include this under the heading of good poetry but it serves a purpose and as well as helping children with mathematical understanding, simple rhymes like this will attune them into rhyming sounds. This is discussed in more detail in the next chapter. Parents and practitioners should be able to use this simple format to write something that fits in with the day-to-day experiences of their children.

## Make a rhyme book

As children become familiar with rhymes, type or write them out with some illustrations, laminate them and make a book of favourites. Children will see the shape of the verses on the page and this will help them to look more closely at word patterns. Older children may trace the words with their fingers as they say the poem and they may be able to spot some of the letters and rhymes. Children in one nursery school have been observed playing out the role of the adult, using the book and 'reading' the poems to a small group of other children.

**FIGURE 3.4** Make a rhyme book to include children's favourite verses. It can be illustrated by hand or with clip art to help children recognise the rhyme. Counting rhymes are always popular.

## Using action rhymes

Action rhymes are another genre loved by young children that also contribute so much to the developmental processes of body coordination, self control, memory and communication. An internet search will bring up a wide selection of CDs which contain many of the well known action rhymes and circle games. Younger children need to respond at their own pace rather than trying to join in a circle game, but as children get older they enjoy the security and fun of holding hands and moving together. Some of the poems in the anthology will lend themselves to simple actions and suggestions are given for these. Some of the action rhymes have been written so they can be sung to a familiar tune and the words reflect something the children have been doing. Look at the example given on page 124: 'This is the way we plant our seeds'. Children could make up verses to this tune to reflect other experiences, e.g. bake a cake, build with bricks, mix our paints, etc. The next poem on page 125, 'What are we going to grow today?' uses another familiar tune and even very young children can follow simple actions as their bodies respond to the beat of the music and the sound of the words.

## Using rhyming and non rhyming poems

Generally speaking we use rhyming verse with younger children rather than non rhyming as it is easier for them to tune in to the patterns. As their vocabulary increases it is important to offer poems that don't rhyme.

The following poems are examples of poems on the same subject but which can be used with children at different stages of language awareness,

### Frogs

*Finger rhyme suitable with children around the age of two. Use actions as suggested or let children make up their own.*

Look down deep in our garden pool,
Down in the water dark and cool (make a circle with arms)
A lump of jelly full of dots
Growing into large black spots (use hands and fingers to make pointed dot
    movements)

Look down deep in our garden pool
Down in the water dark and cool
Spawn has hatched and in a row
The black dots hang and start to grow (hold hands with fingers hanging
    downwards)

Look down deep in our garden pool
Down in the water dark and cool
Big black heads and tails that wiggle
Watch our tadpoles swim and squiggle (fingers move and wriggle)

Look down deep in our garden pool
Down in the water dark and cool
Now the tail is shrinking fast
Four legs growing and at last (make froggy hands)
Baby froglets jumping high
Out of the pool and up to the sky

*(Hands jump up as high as possible. In a smaller group children could pretend to be froglets and jump high. Use the first two lines again if you need to restore a sense of calm and quiet at the end)*

### Frog spawn

*A poem to use with children aged three to five.*

Our garden pool is big and round
You'll never guess what we just found
A lump of shiny jelly dots
Oh so many lots and lots

Then the dots began to grow
Slithered out, hung in a row
Heads grow big and tails wiggle
Watch our tadpoles squirm and squiggle

Back legs grow with froggy toes
The wiggly tail just grows and grows
Then front legs appear at last
The tail gets smaller shrinking fast
Until one day we look around
Tiny frogs hop on the ground

**Tadpoles**

*This poem should be used with children who are confident users of English. It needs to be read aloud fairly slowly in a deliberate manner so each word is given space. As children become familiar with the poem they may be able to discuss some of the structures and the way in which it was written. There are some internal rhymes and some rhyming lines.*

Black dot
One spot
Upon another
Another and another
A slithery, slimy heap
Hanging
Gently upon the weed,
Still
So still,
But then
Black dot
Is not.
Dot becomes comma
Another, another
The growth is fast
Until at last
The comma
Wriggles
Wriggles and pushes
Hatches out
Another, another
Still
They rest so still
On jelly

But soon a tail
Frilly gills
Our tadpoles hang
On weed
So still
So still
For seven days
They love to laze
Then wriggling, jiggling
Curling, whirling
Swimming, prancing
Black tadpoles dancing,
First two back legs
A larger head
We must make sure
They're very well fed.
Front legs grow
Tail shrinks small
Suddenly tadpoles gone
Tiny froglets start
To crawl
Clambering out
One leap, and away
To hide somewhere safe
For the rest of the day

Although these three poems are all about the same experience, their structure means that they are suited to children at different stages of language awareness. The first finger rhyme contains more repetition and by using actions, will engage younger children or children who are learning English. They will learn to join in with the first repeated couplet and do the actions. The second poem uses rhyme but without the repetition and would be suitable for children at a later stage of language and the third poem is more suitable for children who have a good command of English as it is moving away from a rhythmic pattern although it does contain some rhyme. Children may be able to listen for this as they become more familiar with the poem. What is important, however, is that all poems use rich language appropriate to the experience. Even in the first poem the word 'spawn' will reinforce language learning and acquisition of new vocabulary.

## Using poems to support learning experiences

Building poetry into everyday learning is not as difficult as it may sound, once you have the confidence and the resources necessary. As you work with children you may even find yourself making up a short poem with them or one of your own to use. This can often happen as part of children's spontaneous learning. (See forest school case study, on the next page.)

Effective early years practice is a mixture of spontaneous learning, where children create their own learning, and planned learning, where adults build on children's interests and provide opportunities for children to extend their learning. As well as creating or reading a poem 'on the spot' adults can plan to use poetry to support children's experiences and reinforce some of the learning they have just experienced.

Many settings will plant vegetables and flowers in the spring. During the next few months they will be caring for them and harvesting their crops later in the year. When children have finished a particular activity, use one of the poems in this book at the next story time or small group session. This reinforces the learning and also gives them an opportunity to discuss it and hear something that is meaningful to them. Using one of the action songs about planting encourages physical movement and will consolidate some of the actions they may have used whilst planting. There are poems about the four seasons and different types of weather. It is important to involve children with the natural world as much as possible and try to enhance discussions by using a short poem. There are many poems about everyday experiences in the nursery as well as poems to help children with mathematical and literacy skills.

**FIGURE 3.5** Use poetry to support everyday learning experiences such as picking the strawberries.

## Outdoor environment

Outdoor spaces should be planned so that children can interact and have first hand experience of the natural world. In addition to creating small spaces where children can sit and enjoy stories and poems, it is possible to include written texts outdoors which are relevant to children's outdoor learning experiences. A few letters painted on a fence are not as meaningful as some labels which indicate which crop the children are growing, or the role play that is happening in a garden shed. Poems too can be printed, laminated and displayed outdoors.

There should be an area for growing plants and flowers and this could be a natural place for words and poems to be displayed. Plants and vegetables need to be carefully labelled. Children may be able to write their own labels if they are large enough and can often recognise the initial letters and then guess the rest of the word based on their previous knowledge. Similarly a short poem about a plant or particular crop could be laminated and decorated and used as a marker in the flower and vegetable beds.

## Forest school

If you are lucky enough to be able to offer children forest school sessions or something close to this then try to incorporate some songs, poems and verses to enhance the experience.

This can happen spontaneously as in the case study below or be part of the planned experience as children become more aware of the outdoor environment.

---

### Forest school at Peter Pan

Seven children aged three set out for their second forest school session.

Children enthusiastically got their waterproof trousers and wellies on and then were encouraged to pack their own rucksacks with a mat, a mug and a bowl for snacks. The group leader had written a verse for this and used a strong rhythmic beat as she encouraged the children to join in with the verse.

**Our forest school rucksacks**

We're packing our bags for forest school
We're ever so strong, we'll carry it all.
I've got my cup, my bowl my mat,
I need my gloves, I want my hat!!
We're packing our bags for forest school
We're ever so strong we'll carry it all.

---

**FIGURE 3.6** The children have heard the poem about the rucksacks for forest school and are now packing their bags.

Rucksacks on and off they go!

At the first stopping point children had to spot some worms that had escaped (small pieces of wool tied on to branches at different heights. This was to encourage observational skills and all the children were very excited when they found one. Much of this session was exploratory and time was allowed for children to play freely in the woods. They explored with sticks and climbed and balanced on old branches and logs. Towards the end of the session children gathered around the campfire. Currently it is a heap of leaves. The real fire will be lit at a later session once the children understand the rules about using the space safely. After hot chocolate and snacks a leader suggested we sang some campfire songs. Children did not want to sing the traditional ones and one child suggested we sang 'The wheels on the bus'! An adult then started to sing the tune but used the words 'The leaves on the trees are falling down, falling down', etc etc. Then another adult suggested 'The conkers on the tree go plop plop plop'. For the third verse, one adult said, "What sounds do the leaves make as we walk on them? Oliver (whose idea it was to sing "The wheels on the bus" immediately said, 'drizzle drazzle' and the group all sang 'The leaves on the ground go drizzle drazzle, drizzle drazzle,' etc. while Oliver smiled proudly the whole way through the verse.

If this song is sung at future sessions it may become part of their forest school repertoire. This is a good example of using music and words to fit an occasion. As children become used to this they will be able to suggest more ideas of their own using this tune or another familiar tune. On one occasion the weather forecast indicated gales so instead of a structured session the children went for a walk. This involved collecting leaves and sticks and looking closely at them. Children's vocabulary and imagination was extended by adults asking open-ended questions. They discovered puffballs and thought they could be dinosaur eggs. They played in leaves and thought about the sounds they made as they walked through them. They ran, splashed and played in puddles and staff were able to use the poem 'Puddles puddles everywhere' (pages 118–19) when the children returned to the nursery. In this way the poem and its language became part of the learning experience.

**FIGURE 3.7** Run, jump splash: use the poem 'Puddles puddles everywhere' from the anthology after children after been out in the puddles.

On the last session children sat around the campfire and watched it being lit. They were fascinated by this and we talked about the sounds, the smells and sights of the fire before they toasted their marshmallows and buns. After they had eaten we sang a song using words the children had supplied and the tune of 'The wheels on the bus' as we had done previously.

> The smoke on the fire goes wurl swurl wurl etc
> The flames on the fire dance higher and higher
> The sticks on the fire go crackle snazzle pop

We also sang 'Campfire's burning' and listened to the forest school poem (page 153) before tidying up and returning to nursery.

When outside with children it is often much easier to see the world as they are seeing it. It helps us to slow down and appreciate things we may not otherwise notice. Children ask questions about things we have never even thought about. They challenge us and using poems is often a good way to meet that challenge and extend their learning experience as well as offering them a rich language environment.

## Imaginative development

Children between the ages of three and five are beginning to move in imaginary worlds. Role play is important and children will use small world figures to re-enact different scenarios. Poetry can be used to develop their imagination and many poems will take us into a different world. Words are powerful when used well and a good poem will help children to develop mind pictures.

Sometimes children can sit with their eyes closed as you share a poem with them. Encourage them to describe in their own words what they liked about a poem or what they could see in their mind. Sometimes older children may wish to recreate pictures onto paper using whatever medium they wish. Children in reception classes should be able to listen to some well known classic poems, e.g. Wordsworth's famous poem about daffodils (see *The Children's Classic Poetry Collection* listed under 'Books for the children's book box or bookshelf' at the end of this chapter.)

**FIGURE 3.8** Asking children to close their eyes as they listen to a poem develops their imagination.

## Conclusion

Sharing poems with young children can be one of the most rewarding experiences for adults as well as children. Whether it be sharing a book with one child, reading a poem to a small group or working with a large group as they share a rhyme, an action song or listen to a poem together, the shared experience should be enjoyable for everyone.

All children need to hear the sounds and rhythms of any language that is in common use around them. A well chosen poem can often make sense to a child who has little experience of English. They will respond to the rhythm and the pattern structures and may often commit the poem to their memory. This is an important step in their learning of English.

Poetry needs to be everywhere. It needs to be on the walls, on the bookshelf, outside, in the story corner and above all in the minds of the adults as they have conversations and share the experiences of daily life with young children.

## Poetry anthologies

### Books for the adults' bookshelf to share with children: generally without illustrations

*Come into this Poem* Tony Mitton 2011, Frances Lincoln.
A very good anthology to use with children in reception classes. Many poems are based on everyday experiences but there is a growing sense of humour and imagination as the poet explores mythical worlds.

*First Poetry Book, A* Pie Corbett and Gaby Morgan (eds) 2012, Macmillan Children's Books.
An essential book for all settings with children in Foundation Stage. There are so many poems in this collection which recount the everyday experiences of young children in a way that they can understand and enjoy. Adults too will enjoy reading these poems aloud and sharing them with children. The topics are fairies, mermaids and princesses; mythical creatures and dinosaurs; transport; pets and animals; families; seasons and weather; school; people who help us; pirates; the senses; space; feelings; wildlife; minibeasts; food; where we live; nature; friends and the past. There are so many poems in this collection which can be used alongside the learning experiences of children. The section on feelings offers scaffolding for discussions around personal social and emotional development.

*Orange Silver Sausage: A Collection of Poems Without Rhymes* compiled by Carter and Denton 2009, Walker Books.
A wonderful collection of poems showing how poetry does not rely on rhyme but on carefully chosen words positioned so they create pictures in the mind or recall familiar situations. Lots of humour too and play on words which will appeal to

five-year-olds. Some poems in this collection are more suitable for older children but try 'Mr Khan's shop', and 'A dictionary of snow' and 'The Rev Spooner's shopping list' for its wonderful play on words and reversal of first letters – this is a good one to encourage children's listening and reading skills. Children will enjoy learning the meaning of the word 'spoonerisms' and are sure to remember it if they hear the poem as well. Rev. W. A. Spooner was an Oxford academic who often would get his words muddled using the initial of one word and transposing it to another and the Greek word for this is metathesis.

*Puffin Book of Fantastic First Poems, A* June Crebbin (ed.) 2000, Puffin.
There is an abridged version of this book under the title *The Booktime Book of Fantastic First Poems* June Crebbin (ed.) 2008.

*The Works Key Stage 1* chosen by Pie Corbett 2014, Macmillan Children's Books.
Although this book is titled Key Stage 1, I would recommend it for all Foundation Stage settings. The first section nursery rhymes contains many of the more unusual rhymes that we may have forgotten about but which are still part of our heritage and which we probably heard as children. Similarly the next section contains a comprehensive list of circle songs, again familiar titles but many of which we may not have used for some years.

Two further sections, 'Action rhymes' and 'Songs and counting rhymes', both have a very good selection for children from the age of two upwards. Having this book to hand will help practitioners to be more adventurous and use a wider variety of short songs and rhymes at the end of the day as well as in structured circle time or group sessions. At the back of the book there are instructions for how to use the games and rhymes with groups. There is a good selection of poems to use with older children on the animal world and the natural world.

Further sections in the book contain a wide range of poems to use with children of four or five maybe in a reception class. Children and adults alike will love the tongue twisters and these can be built into the planning for children's literacy. Dip into the book for yourself and you will have so many lovely poems to share with the children it will be difficult to know where to start.

*This Little Puffin: A Treasury of Nursery Rhymes, Songs and Games* revised edition 1992, Puffin.
This was the book I began with and even now I still use it. It has just so many poems that will appeal to children from babies to five-year-olds. There is a wide variety of subjects and also games and songs to enjoy.

## Collections for the children's book box or bookshelf

*100 Best Poems for Children* Roger McGough (ed.) 2001, Puffin Poetry.
Another well illustrated book which will appeal to children from four onwards.

*Children's Classic Poetry Collection, The* 2013, Armadillo Books.
This book is beautifully illustrated and contains classic poems by many of our

greatest poets. Some of them are more suitable for older children but some like Wordsworth's 'Daffodils', Edward Lear's 'The owl and the pussy cat', or a traditional nursery rhyme such as 'Hush little baby' can be enjoyed by children in Foundation Stage. Children will enjoy just hearing the rhymes and the sound patterns in other poems.

*Hey Little Bug*: *Poems for Little Creatures* James Carter 2011, Frances Lincoln.
Definitely a must have book for all settings. Contains good poems about the creatures and minibeasts that children find and love to observe. The poems are well written and suitable for children from the age of three.

*Macmillan Treasury of Nursery Rhymes and Poems, The* Alison Green (ed.) with a foreword by Roger McGough and illustrated by Anna Currey 1998, MacMillan Children's Books.
This is definitely one of my very favourite anthologies and should be available in every setting. It is a really good one to recommend to parents and if you can afford a few copies make it available for them to borrow for a week. Children will love looking at the illustrations as they snuggle up even if they don't understand all the words. They will feel strong rhythms and hear some rhyme. The book is divided into sections. A few of these are poems for the garden, weather poems, poems about me, farmyard poems, action rhymes, counting poems, wild animals, town. This is an essential part of a child's literary heritage.

*Machine Poems, Noisy Poems, Seaside Poems, Tasty Poems*: Four books of poems collected by Jill Bennett and illustrated by Nick Sharratt 2007 (paperback), Oxford University Press.
Another set for the poetry box or shelf. These paperbacks are again brightly illustrated and will appeal to children from the age of three. Lots of these poems are just great fun and an adult can have has much enjoyment as the children as they encourage them to join in. There are poems too from the Caribbean.

*Mad About Minibeasts* Giles Andreae and David Wojtowycz 2011, Orchard Books.
This should be on the poetry shelf or in the poetry box in all settings. It is brightly illustrated and comes in a large, hardback version. Pictures will appeal to children of a very young age and will help them concentrate as they hear the poems and become involved in this book. There is a poem for every minibeast which is commonly found in the garden. The poems are short, easy to understand and well written. They all use rhyme and there is plenty of alliteration and rich language.

*Mother Goose Nursery Rhymes* edited by Axel Scheffler 2010 Pan MacMillan Children's Books. Short stories link the rhymes and the book is nicely illustrated. It contains a good selection of traditional nursery rhymes but no music so a good one if you know the tunes already and need reminding of some of the words. Can be used at home or with a small group.

*Mulberry Collection First Book of Children's Rhymes, The* words by Patricia Irvine artwork by Kate Scurfield 2011, Peninsular One Source.

A beautifully illustrated book to share with children – poems about everyday experiences. Use this with children from the age of four.

*Poems for the Very Young* selected by Michael Rosen and illustrated by Bob Graham, 1996, Kingfisher.
Another beautifully illustrated book that will appeal to adults and children alike. A good range of poems suitable for use with children of different ages so they can use the book for many years!

*Poetry Paintbox* poems chosen by John Foster 1995, Hachette Children's books.
This is a set of anthologies: orange, green, yellow, purple, blue and red suitable for children aged four and over. They may be out of print but old copies can be bought on Amazon and they contain a good selection of poems on various themes like colours, numbers, shapes and sizes and letters of the alphabet.

*Read Aloud Rhymes for the Very Young* Jack Prelutsky (ed.) 1986, Knopf Publishing.
Beautifully illustrated book –great for parents and children to share together.

*Under the Moon – Over the Sea* a collection of poetry from the Caribbean John Ayard and Grace Nicholas (eds) 2011, Walker Books London.
This collection has brilliant poems with very rich use of language, some in Caribbean dialect but can be used with all children. The section 'Come taste and buy' has some very evocative poems describing fruits and foods. Find the good poem here about a pineapple. The last poem in the collection 'Goodbye granny' is particularly relevant for families who may live in the UK yet spend a lot of time travelling to and from their homes in their Caribbean.

*Wriggle and Roar Rhymes to Join in with* words byJulia Donaldson illustrated by Nick Sharratt 2011, MacMillan Children's Books.
A big book version is ideal but this is also available in paperback.

**PLATE 1.01** Many libraries offer rhyme time sessions. This baby is eleven weeks old and has not only managed to stay awake for the whole session but is focusing intently on the group leader as she listens to the rhymes and songs.

**PLATE 1.02** Mothers and babies enjoy poetry and song at a musical bumps session.

**PLATE 1.03** Toddlers enjoy using musical instruments to accompany nursery rhymes at a musical bumps session.

**PLATE 1.04** Poetry friendly spaces can be made inside and out. This tepee is used for rhymes, stories and poetry.

**PLATE 1.05** A pop up tent is a cheaper option than a tepee and is useful for settings that need to clear away each session. Make it welcoming and attractive with books and toys.

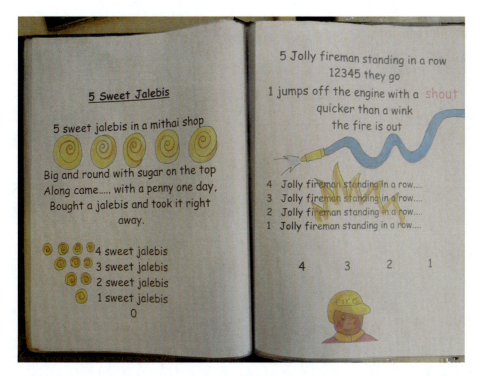

5 Jolly fireman standing in a row
12345 they go
1 jumps off the engine with a shout
quicker than a wink
the fire is out

4 Jolly fireman standing in a row....
3 Jolly fireman standing in a row....
2 Jolly fireman standing in a row....
1 Jolly fireman standing in a row....

4     3     2     1

fire

5 Sweet Jalebis

5 sweet jalebis in a mithai shop

Big and round with sugar on the top
Along came..... with a penny one day,
Bought a jalebis and took it right
away.

4 sweet jalebis
3 sweet jalebis
2 sweet jalebis
1 sweet jalebis
0

**PLATE 1.06** Make a rhyme book. It can contain traditional nursery rhymes as well as favourite poems and counting rhymes.

**PLATE 1.07** Cara used this rhyme book with great understanding and her small group listened and joined in for over fifteen minutes.

**PLATE 1.08** Olivia uses the rhyme book every day. Here she is leading an impromptu nursery rhyme session as she sings 'One, two, three, four, five, once I caught a fish alive'.

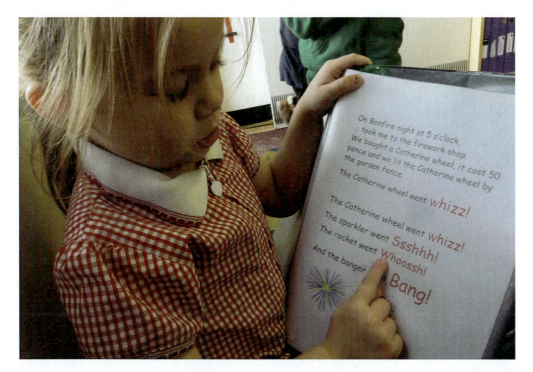

On Bonfire night at 5 o'clock,
... took me to the firework shop.
We bought a Catherine wheel, it cost 50
pence and we lit the Catherine wheel by
the garden fence.

The Catherine wheel went whizz!

The Catherine wheel went whizz!
The sparkler went Ssshhh!
The rocket went Whoossh!
And the banger ... Bang!

**PLATE 1.09** Here Olivia uses the rhyme book on her own as she picks out the words printed in red thereby developing her reading skills.

**PLATE 1.10** Children's interest in this caterpillar was extended as they listened to the caterpillar poem outside after they had finished observing it.

**PLATE 1.11** Children at Crosfield created their poems in a special space under the blossom tree.

**PLATE 1.12** Morgan studies the leaf closely before joining in the group to create a poem about autumn leaves.

**PLATE 1.13 & 1.14** After listening to an autumn poem children created their poem about leaves. Penelope enjoyed illustrating it and Olivia and Rosie enjoyed leaf play outdoors.

**PLATE 1.15** Children at Peter Pan enjoyed the puddles and then listened to the poem 'Puddles': run, jump and splash.

**PLATE 1.16** Children at Peter Pan sit around the campfire and sing songs, sometimes making up their own versions.

# Sharing poetry as part of children's literacy development

Many parents and practitioners are very aware that using poems and rhymes is an excellent way to help children understand letter sounds. However, it must be stressed that if children have already been used to hearing poems and rhymes on a regular basis from birth onwards, this process will seem very much more relevant and enjoyable. Poetry should be enjoyed for its own sake initially and then it may be useful in helping children with early reading. This chapter gives some suggestions and examples of ways to help children with letters and sounds. The Bookstart website states very clearly that dramatic benefits to literacy are to be gained from exposure to rhymes. The website listed at the end of this chapter states that:

> *Evidence suggests that a familiarity with rhymes helps children to detect the phonetic constituents of words. Children at a very young age can recognise that cat rhymes with mat. In making this connection, they detect the word segment 'at'. Because rhyming words – words that have sounds in common – often share spelling sequences in their written form, children sensitive to rhymes are well equipped to develop their reading. By making children aware that words share segments of sounds (e.g. the -ight segment shared by light, fight, and might), rhymes help prepare them to learn that such words often have spelling sequences in common too.*
>
> *(Goswami 1986, 1988)*

> *A child that has learnt this characteristic of rhyme is therefore likely to be well equipped to learn how certain spellings produce similar-sounding words once they start school.*
>
> *Experience suggests that when they begin to learn reading, children that are sensitive to rhyme are better able to make the inference, for example, that fight and might are likely to be spelt the same way as the word light. In this way, learning to read one new word is readily extended to learning several more. Singing rhymes at the toddler stage therefore provides a strong foundation for learning to read later on. Put simply, good rhymers make good readers!*
>
> *(www.bookstart.org.uk/professionals/about-bookstart-and-the-packs/research/*
> *reviews-and-resources/the-benefit-of-rhymes/)*

## Evidence and outcomes

A number of longitudinal studies confirm this thesis and indicate that knowledge of rhymes helps children progress in reading once they start school. For example, studies have demonstrated that the better children are at detecting rhymes the quicker and more successful they will be at learning to read (Bradley 1988c, Bradley and Bryant, 1983, Ellis and Large, 1987).

## Poems and rhyming stories

Using a short poem or verse when children are very young is an excellent introduction to listening to rhyming sounds.

Children will soon learn to discriminate and when they become more fluent in speaking they will enjoy the wonderful variety of rhyming stories that are now available. Julia Donaldson has written many books suitable for use with toddlers as well as children between the ages of three and five. Her story books, *Sharing a Shell*, *What the Ladybird Heard* and *What the Ladybird Heard Next*, are well illustrated and children will become aware of the words and should be able to join in as they get to know the story. Her book *The Rhyming Rabbit* is particularly suitable for using with children who are ready for some more directed work on rhyme. The rhymes in the rabbit's poems are sometimes very obvious but sometimes there are subtle hidden inner rhymes embedded in rich descriptive and narrative language. She has also written a set of phonics books 'Songbirds phonics', a well thought-out approach to reading where the child will become involved with the characters in the story as well as learning the skills of reading.

## Letters and sounds

In 2007 the government produced guidelines for working with young children to help them with early stages of reading. The document 'Letters and sounds' is still widely used today and is based on recognising that children are individuals and need a broad, balanced, high quality curriculum. It gives suggestions of how to work with children using the environment both indoors and out and by suggesting a range of activities that fit in with effective early years practice. I would suggest, however, that there could be much more emphasis on using poetry and have listed some suggestions for poems which can be used to support each of the first six aspects of Phase One. This section applies mainly to practitioners but there is no reason at all why parents should not also use some of the following ideas.

### Aspect 1: general sound discrimination

The listening walk suggested here is an excellent way of encouraging small children to listen to the sounds around them. Any outdoor space can be used even if you cannot go for a walk. Children who are reaching the end of Foundation Stage should be able to make lots of suggestions and with some adult support may be able to write a poem about what they hear. (See ideas in Chapter 5.)

Some of the poems in this book are written to include the five senses and if children become familiar with these poems try to use the verse about sounds to encourage them to see if they can hear these sounds for themselves when they go out.

> What did you hear in the garden today?
> As you ran outside eager to play?
> My friends shouting, a laugh and a cry
> An aeroplane engine high in the sky
> But the most wonderful sound I ever heard
> Was the deep throated song of a tiny bird.
> The rustle of grasses waving in the breeze
> And the wind as it rustles through all the leaves
> Soft fall of rain on the roof and the ground
> Leaves crunching, frogs croaking – a wonderful sound.

Encourage children to hear not only the everyday sounds but anything special that might only be heard during a particular season of the year.

> When I go out I hear autumn
> Leaves crunching
> High winds in the tree
> And twittering of migrating birds

Bonfire night is always a good time for children to talk about what they hear outside.

> What can you hear on a dark winter's night?
> Fireworks crackling and whooshing,
> Red gold and white.

The poems in the weather section include some about the sounds of the wind and thunderstorms. 'Autumn winds', page 108 describes the wind in different moods, blowing, roaring, whistling and whispering. Children may like to stamp and scrunch through the leaves as suggested in the last line of this poem. The poem 'Wind in the town' describes the wind whistling down the street. On a windy day, ask the children which word they think best describes the wind. Are there any noises that are directly caused by the wind? Encourage children to listen to leaves blowing in the breeze or in a strong wind.

The book *Noisy Poems* by Jill Bennett, illustrated by Nick Sharratt is an excellent one to use to help children listen. 'Fishes evening song' describes the sound of the water and uses rich vocabulary and good poetic structure. It is an excellent example of a non rhyming poem suitable to use with younger children.

## Aspect 2: instrumental sounds

All children should have access to a wide range of musical instruments that can be shaken or hit to create a wide variety of sounds. Instruments should be available both indoors and outdoors.

Instruments can range from tuned percussion to simple homemade shakers. In addition to the suggestions made in the 'Letters and sounds' document, use instruments to accompany some of the poems as you read them as well as more traditional nursery rhymes. The poem 'Musical instruments' in *Noisy Poems* can be used with very young children as well as children who are much older. Also try reading the poems 'The ceremonial band' and 'The jazz man' from the same book. Each instrument has been given a word sound and children can mime playing these or even better use their own instruments to accompany the poem. The link between music and poetry is strong. Sometimes poems are read against a musical background. Sometimes music may inspire a poem and sometimes it is the other way round. There is now a poetry competition run by the BBC for poems that have been inspired by a particular piece of music played during the Prom concerts.

**FIGURE 4.1** Musical instruments should be available outside. If you don't have a designated space like this use a basket or box in a secluded corner.

## Aspect 3: body percussion

In Chapter 2 there are many suggestions for using poems with babies that involve touching different parts of the body. Rhythms of clapping and rocking should be used as much as possible with very small children and children from the age of 18 months will enjoy a variety of finger rhymes. As they gain more control over their own body movements they will be able to use different parts of their body in different ways to keep a steady beat.

Use 'The body rhyme' from Chapter 2 and then introduce 'Heads, shoulders, knees and toes.' 'The puddle poem', page 153 can be used with actions as children run, jump and splash'. Physical action is a good way to internalise rhyme and will help children to remember a poem and consequently help them with remembering letter sounds. Use a rap poem such as 'Jasper's bean', page 100. The poem 'Summertime', page 100 can also be read with a strong rap rhythm and children can move or clap or both as they learn the poem.

The poem 'Dinosaur' can also be used to encourage children to move in different ways and it contains some exciting vocabulary for them to try out too, pages 182–3.

The poem 'Wind around my body' is an excellent one to raise awareness of different parts of the body. Use the suggestions for movement printed with the poem on page 122.

## Aspect 4: rhythm and rhyme

The *Letters and Sounds* guidance states clearly on page 29 that children need to build a stock of rhymes through hearing them repeated over and over again. It is, however, important not to repeat the same ones until the children are bored, and to remember to include some new ones as well. Try using poems as well as the more traditional rhymes. The poem 'Song of the train' in *Noisy Poems* (details in the section, Collections for the children's book box or bookshelf at the end of Chapter 3) is a simple poem with a very strong rhythm and will hold the attention of children from the age of two. For children learning English as an additional language, songs and rhymes help them to tune into the rhythm and sounds of English. The suggestion to compile a book of favourite rhymes is one which is referred to in more detail in the previous chapter of this book. In addition to the activities described in the Letters and sounds document you might like to try the following. One of the suggestions in the document is to 'encourage children's word play by inventing new rhymes'. The case study below is based on this suggestion using the nursery rhyme 'Hickory dickory dock'.

---

**Crosfield Nursery Group, Aim: to listen to, and begin to use rhyming words**

Sylvie has a group of six children all with English as a first language. She has been talking to them about rhyming words and has been using rhyming stories. Today she has an illustrated template in large print of the nursery rhyme 'Hickory dickory dock' with some spaces for children to use their own rhyming words.

She reads the original poem first using a large nursery rhyme book and then asks the group to give a different word instead of 'dock'. They came up with the following verses

---

**FIGURE 4.2** Children are enjoying making their own rhymes based on the traditional nursery rhyme 'Hickory dickory dock'.

Hickory dickory bee
The mouse ran up a tree
Hickory dickory pop
The mouse went to the shop
He bought some cheese
He said yes please
Hickory dickory pop.

The group then listened to the story, *Where's my Ted*? and Sylvie asked them to listen and say when they could hear a rhyme. Most children could hear the more obvious rhymes but maybe not the hidden ones. As they were intent on the story they became more involved in the plot and three children gave different suggestions as to the outcome of the story.

Sylvie commented that the group was making good progress on rhyme recognition but since I had been going in she had become very much more aware of the importance of building poetry into the daily routine and was trying to include more, particularly in her group story times.

## Creating rhymes with children

If children have been used to hearing rhyming poems on a regular basis they will soon become very good at finding their own rhymes. If poems are used on a regular basis children can often supply the word at the end of the line particularly in a rhyming couplet. An example of this is seen in this extract from 'The beach bag', page 99.

> Here is a bucket, fill it with sand
> Pat it down carefully with the palm of your hand
> Here is a spade shiny and new
> I can dig in the sand and so can you
> We can make a castle or dig a deep hole
> A sand car a dinosaur or even a mole
> Here is the sun cream, it's kept out of reach
> But we always use it when out on the beach
> Rub on your arms your legs and your nose
> Your tummy your feet and even your toes

In the next poem there is a different rhyming pattern which is referred to as ABAB. The rhymes are seen at the end of alternate lines. This is more difficult for children as they have to listen and remember longer chunks of language. They will also get help from the clue given in line 3 of the poem 'Shopping' (full poem on page 186).

> I decided to go to the pet shop
> I thought I'd buy a snake
> But I ended up in the bakers
> And so I bought a cake
>
> I decided to go the bakers
> Because I needed some bread
> But I ended up in the butchers
> And bought some meat instead

Encourage children to listen to the sounds of their names. Use the poem 'Names' on page 185 and ask if they can find a word that rhymes with their names. As children become more adept at this, it may be possible in a small group to compile some verses rather like the poem.

Use a simple format such as the one below. Children at Crosfield came up with their versions.

> When I was two I said goo goo
> When I was three I ran to the sea
> When I was four I had a big roar
> When I was five I sat on a hive
> When I was six I broke my lip
> When I was seven I flew to Devon

When I was eight I fixed the gate
When I was nine I listened to the chimes
When I was ten I wrote with a pen

When I was two I sat on a shoe
When I was three I turned a key
When I was four I sat on a claw
When I was 5 I swim and dive
When I was 6 a ball I kicked
When I was 7 I was hot in heaven
When I was 8 I was late
When I was nine I was kind
When I was 10 I watched Ben ten

## Aspect 5: alliteration

Alliteration is a common feature of good poetry and can be found in many poems. Read 'The yak' by Jack Prelustsky in *Noisy Poems* (details in Useful additional resources at the end of this chapter).

A good way to introduce children to alliteration might be to read the animal alphabet poem (page 181). They could perhaps go on to create some other short lines about different animals. Using names is also a good way to begin and the poem on pages 184–5 provides another useful starting point. Again children should be encouraged to think of words with the same initial letters as their own names. If possible try to work with small groups rather than a whole class for any of these exercises.

Use a story book such as 'Lullaby Lion', which uses a lot of alliteration. Younger children enjoy this just as a story but older children will be able to hear the sounds and the way they are used. This can be used as a basis for encouraging children to think of a different animal and some alliterative words to describe it. Children at Crosfield came up with the following examples.

'Slithery snake slippery snake'

They then added

'snakey snake, shakey snake, sliding snake and slimy snake.'

This could be printed out as a poem in its own right. They went on to add

'small snake, super snake, sleeping snake and scary snake.'

The next animal they thought of was a hedgehog and they suggested;

'a happy hopping hedgehog' and 'a horrid hairy hedgehog'.

## Aspect 6: voice sounds

The main purpose of the activities in this section is to explore speech sounds and talk about different sounds we can make with our voices. Poetry is the perfect way to extend some of the suggestions in the document and at the same time offers a rich curriculum. Reading a poem well makes demands on the adult reader. The voice should be used in different ways to lend meaning and maybe give emphasis to different words. Just as in storytelling, different characters in a poem should be given different voice sounds. In a poem such as 'Ants' (pages 136–7) children can learn the lines in speech marks and use their own voices to create the characters in the poem. Can they make a snail voice to use in the poem 'The snail'?

Poems such as Lucy's first poem about the rain stick (Chapter 5, page 77) uses sounds such as whoosh and swoosh. As children play they can be encouraged to use voice sounds and they should be able to use them as they hear poems, particularly about the wind, the rain or a thunder storm. Use the poem 'Autumn winds' (page 108) to help children to discriminate between the different sounds the wind can make.

## Aspect 7: Oral blending and segmenting

If children have become attuned to rhyme, rhythm and alliteration then they are in a good place to begin to use the poetry cards suggested by Bruce and Spratt in *Essentials of Literacy* (Sage 2011).

A simple, well known nursery rhyme is printed out on card and the card may be illustrated and laminated. The authors give a detailed breakdown of the ways in which children use these to build up experience of strategies for early reading but

**FIGURE 4.3** Olivia is reciting the poem in the rhyme book from memory but she is also following the words with her fingers. She is learning about how letters and words make meaning.

also stress the importance of engaging with the seven aspects in *Letters and Sounds* within the four principles of the framework of the Early Years Foundation Stage. (A unique child, positive relationships, enabling environments and development and learning.) This needs to be emphasised again and if poetry is built into to an effective early years curriculum, then the ideas above will come as a natural way of helping children to engage in the literacy curriculum. The advice offered by Dunst et al. (2011) for younger children cannot be bettered. They suggest that adults should 'identify the nursery rhymes and rhyming games that the young child especially enjoys and actively engage the child in the activities as part of routine play'.

Children will also enjoy using a rhyme book as suggested in Chapter 3 and this is another informal way to help link the letters with the sounds as they know many of the poems and rhymes by heart.

## Conclusion

The most important conclusion to be drawn from this chapter is based on the evidence quoted in the Bookstart leaflets and website. If a child has been hearing poetry and rhyme from an early age, this can have a dramatic impact on a child's ability to learn to read. He will have been enjoying stories and poems and hopefully this sense of enjoyment and fun can be sustained as he tries to come to terms with the complexities of the written word. Children are nowadays often subject to formal teaching of phonics from a very young age. Some children will not necessarily be at a developmental stage that is appropriate and will really struggle. Children in reception year are given formal phonics teaching and many of these children will have been born in the summer months and will only be four years old. Children need to have as much play based experience in their early years and hopefully the fun and enjoyment of poetry will support this style of learning. Children need to be active learners. Action rhymes, poems with strong rhythms and poems that can be used with music, will all encourage this learning style. Rhyming stories too can be a useful resource as children should be able to concentrate and really enjoy longer stories. Poems should be used too however, as they will help to develop the child's own imagination without the help of the illustrations that accompany the stories. A lively imagination is important for the creative process of making poems as we discover in the next chapter.

## Useful additional resources

*Lullaby Lion* by Vivian French and Alison Bartlett 2003, Walker Books.
*Noisy Poems* collected by Jill Bennett, illustrated by Nick Sharratt 1987 Oxford University Press.
Dr. Seuss books. Many books but a good starting point is the 'Beginners collection' published 2009 by Random House.

Julia Donaldson stories and reading books. Look at her website for a complete list www.juliadonaldson.co.uk

## References

Bradley, L. (1988). 'Rhyme recognition and reading and spelling in young children', In R. L. Masland and M. R. Masland (eds), *Pre-school Prevention of Reading Failure*. Parkton, MD: York Press.

Bradley, L. and Bryant, P. E. (1983). 'Categorizing sounds and learning to read: a causal connection', *Nature*, 30, 419-421.

Bruce T. and Spratt J. (2011) *Essentials of Literacy from 0–7*. Sage Publications.

Department for Education and Skills (DfES) (2007) *Letters and Sounds: Principles and Practice of High Quality Phonics*. London: DfES.

Dunst, C. J., Meter, D. and Hamby, D. W. (2011) Review in *Centre for Early Literacy Learning (CELL)* Vol. 4, No. 1.

Ellis, N. and Large, B. (1987). 'The development of reading: as you seek you shall find', *British Journal of Psychology*, 1, 329–342.

Goswami, U. (1986) 'Children's use of analogy in learning to read: A developmental study', *Journal of Experimental Child Psychology*, 42, 73–83.

Goswami, U. (1988) 'Children's use of analogy in learning to spell', *British Journal of Developmental Psychology*, 6, 21–34.

www.bookstart.org.uk/professionals/about-bookstart-and-the-packs/research/reviews-and-resources/the-benefit-of-rhyme/

# Creating poetry with young children

*I have never started a poem whose end I knew. Writing a poem is discovering.*

(*Robert Frost*)

Embarking on a poetry journey with very young children can be exciting and fulfilling for everyone involved. Young children will often make up small poems, songs and chants spontaneously as they play. If children grow up in an environment where music, song and rhyme is something that happens every day, they will become aware of the fundamental nature of poetry as an expressive art form. Poetry is closely linked to song, and the nursery rhymes we use with babies are part of a long tradition. Poetry itself has been an art form for thousands of years. It is important that we offer children the chance to develop some sense of this tradition and hopefully they in turn will pass this on to their own children. This chapter offers suggestions of how to support and encourage children to create their own poems. Children often think that rhyme is an essential component of a poem and sometimes they need help to understand that a poem does not need to rhyme. There are suggestions for helping children with this and the chapter is illustrated with case studies and examples of creating poetry with children from three to five. Using children's first hand learning experience is the best way to start and as children become more used to the idea of creating their poems they will be able to use them not only to support learning but extend their creative and imaginative powers. The chapter ends with some examples of different styles of poems which are particularly suitable to use with children in reception classes.

## Poetry making should be fun

The most important thing to remember is that any form of poetry making should be fun, both for the adults and the children involved. In this chapter, the focus is on helping children use words to create poems and it is not about activities to help them to understand rhymes or phonic sounds. Children should be enjoying the vocabulary they have learnt and creating poetry is a way to help children extend and experiment with language. Rhymes may pop up spontaneously or they may not. Children should be encouraged to listen to the sounds of the words they are using but adults need to be flexible in their approach and this will be a new learning experience for everyone involved. I have used the term creating or making rather than writing as older children in reception classes may feel inhibited if they regard this as an exercise in writing. What is important is that it is a verbal experience and an adult should be ready to scribe the children's ideas. Children's first poems are usually a string of descriptive words. Sometimes they use onomatopoeic words as seen in Lucy's poem on page 77 about the rain stick. Repetition often occurs and children should be encouraged to use words in different ways.

## Where do we start?

If you are hoping to create poems with your children then it is probably true that poetry is beginning to be part of their everyday learning experience. It is a good idea at some point to spend some time reflecting on how much poetry the children hear every day or within a week. It is likely that there will be more than you first thought. Most children will have heard rhyming stories, nursery rhymes and songs but hopefully after reading the previous chapters you will now be thinking of ways to extend your own repertoire and make poetry an integral part of the everyday routines.

Confident adults will inspire confident children, so don't be afraid of asking children to make poems. Poetry is about developing language and promoting enjoyment of words. It is another way to share words with friends and adults. If adults are sharing poems with children on a regular basis, children will soon want to create and share their poems too.

## Enjoying poetry

It is important that adults enjoy poems themselves and if you are feeling hesitant about this, try to spend some time looking through some poems either for yourself or for the children. Some of the poems in the anthologies listed at the end of Chapter 3 are so exciting you will feel the need to share them with the children and as the repertoire builds up so will your confidence. Inspiring children to create their own poems is not that difficult. Children need to know that poems do not need to rhyme, but that they contain exciting words and can be about absolutely anything. (See Useful resources at the end of this chapter, *It Doesn't Have to Rhyme Katie*.)

# Starting from scratch: using children's first hand experiences

### Peter Pan Preschool: the chicks

When first asked about using poetry in the setting, the manager said she didn't think it was something that they did very much and was uncertain about it, but thought it might it might be quite good to do a bit more. The staff discussed this and realised they used far more poems, rhymes and verses than they realised. One member of staff was interested to explore this in more depth and as part of her performance management decided she would look more closely at the way children were using language and focus on asking them to think about the words they used and possibly creating some poems. Staff felt strongly it needed to be related to children's first hand experience and as they were observing baby chicks on a daily basis that might be a good place to start. She asked the children to look closely at the chicks and describe a few features. She used questions such as, 'What might they eat? 'What do you think they are feeling? What is it like when you touch one? She wrote down the ideas and the children re read them with her and created a poetic structure. The following poems were created over two sessions.

These are the 'have a go' poems about the chicks. The first is from group work on a Monday morning at nursery.

> A chicken what's a chicken?
> Well didn't you know?
> They look like chickens
> With stripes on their backs
> They are yellow and fluffy
> Their eyes are black.
> They are wriggly with feathers
> They peck with their beaks
> They do pooh, drink water, they have claws on their feet!

Khaydn's description:

> Chicken eating pizza
> And meeting a cat
> Walking into space, all bundled up with keys
> And strawberries, and lemons and lemons and lemons.

Gus's story:

> A chick ate a pizza with nothing on it – no sauce, no cheese, no salami, he forgot all about the toppings. He just ate raw pizza, nothing more! He went back to the shop, flying through the sky, bumped into a cloud and fell all the way to the floor.

Elliot's poem:

> A chicken on a treasure hunt in Waterers Woods
> Saw X marks the spot and dug all he could
> Discovered a treasure chest with jewels of all kinds
> Back home to Knaphill, so rich with his finds.

Jessica's poem:

> Black eyes
> Yellow wings
> Smelly feet
> Poop on the grass
> Poop on their feet
> Poop on their legs
> Catch flies with their beaks
> Chomp, chomp, chomp.

Oscar W, Tom E and Luke:

> No black noses
> Just yellow beaks
> Claws for toeses
> No chocolate to eat.

The poems show an awareness of language and flow in a way that is different from ordinary sentences. Some children moved into an imaginary world and one child used his own experiences of going on treasure hunts in the local woods to create his poem.

The poems have a vivid and strong quality which can only be produced by first hand experiences.

Staff felt more confident and wanted to go on to encourage children to write poems about a Minotaur. This was in connection with an ongoing project where children visited a local arts group and saw a sculpture of the Minotaur and heard the story. They have explored in depth the movements of the Minotaur and created their own model. They are building a maze with wood and nails. Children had described the Minotaur in sentence form only up until that point so staff were interested to see whether they could create poems too.

The whole project was been documented with photographs and became an in depth project involving all aspects of creativity. It seemed natural following the success of poetry about chicks for staff to include poetry as part of the project.

## Peter Pan Preschool: the Minotaur

**FIGURE 5.1** Children at Peter Pan made a model of the Minotaur and wrote their poems about him.

Two weeks after writing the poems about chicks the children finished their Minotaur sculpture and created the maze with wood nails and string. Kathy, the project leader, asked children to think of a password for a maze. They came up with words such as 'magic o magic, abracadabra, cookie cake, sunshine, chocolate, raindrop, snowflake and beetle'. The children were then able to work as a group to write this poem:

**The Minotaur in the maze**

He lives in a maze
His horns are pointy
He is loads scary.

His nails are sharp
He has a fast face
His hands are curly.

He has sharp teeth
He has yellow teeth (he doesn't clean them).

He has horns and big feet
He looks like a bear
Growling, loudly growling.

He's bigger than a pirate ship
As big as a giant or a dinosaur
Bigger than a tree that's really tall
He can leap like a cannon ball!

He would be grumpy, but he's just too grumpy.
He is a bit grumpy because he's hungry.

He says roar
He goes raaarrrrr
When he eats people he won't be grumpy anymore.

This case study shows how the adult is able to use her own enthusiasm to inspire the children and how the language used is an integral part of the children's learning experiences. It cannot be separated and the new words and structures that children hear will become embedded in their own language vocabulary and skills. Asking children to think of a password is an exciting way to encourage them and unlock their creativity. As Kathy said the poem initially started off by being a bit static but by asking some appropriate, open-ended questions she was able to encourage them to come up with some really imaginative ideas. Kathy's comment was that she was 'ridiculously excited' by the children's work.

This study shows too how staff can become involved. Having initially thought that they didn't do much, the staff moved on and became empowered to inspire children to create poems like this. Poetry sharing and creating is now much more part of their everyday learning together.

## Spontaneous poems

Children as young as three will be able to use sound words to describe everyday things. They may sometimes make up their own little chants and jingles as they play together. Sometimes if an adult is listening and maybe just asks an appropriate question, a child will respond with poetic language.

Listening to the bath water running out, inspired Louise to say,

*'Gurgle glub, gurgle glub, its gone down the plug.'*

Being aware of what the children are saying often can lead to children being able to make up a poem or song as they play.

Children playing with large blocks often create their own scenario, maybe going to the moon or building a fire engine or a racing car. In one nursery a group of children was sitting inside the blocks they had used to create a bus. As they sat there the adult joined in their play and they began to sing to the tune of Lord of the dance. The adult asked the children where they were going and helped with the rhyming structure but the vocabulary and ideas were supplied by the children. The poem was printed out and used during story session for several days after that. Some children were able to learn the words as they had been so involved in it. The poem is included in the anthology in the section 'Life at Nursery', page 151.

## Making up an action song together

Using a familiar tune and setting words to it is an easy way to begin. It is important when working with a group of children, that they are familiar with the experience you will be writing about. This can very often happen spontaneously as children are playing together as in the example below.

*Talk to the children about a recent experience. It could be painting, cooking or going out in the garden. Use the tune to 'The wheels on the bus' (this idea came from a child, see forest school study in Chapter 3, pages 137–8). You can start off by making up the first verse yourself.*

E.g. We're going in the garden to have a look around, have a look around, have a look around. We're going in the garden to have a look around, on this sunny morning. (Make this appropriate to the weather that day e.g. windy rainy snowy etc.)

Maybe you can ask the children what creatures they can find in the garden.

If they say a worm you will need to add another syllable to fit in with the tune so ask them to describe the worm.

E.g. We saw a slippery earthworm crawling on the ground, crawling on the ground etc.

Stop again and ask another question.

What other word would be better than crawling, maybe 'slithering' along the ground.

In the same way introduce adjectives and verbs.

We saw a robin redbreast hopping all round, hopping all around etc.

We saw a fluffy squirrel eating nuts he'd found.

Although the suggestions above all end in the same rhyme this does not have to happen. In this way you are inviting them to begin to think about the words they are using and make choices. As they become familiar with this, their vocabulary increases but also so does their sense of word appropriateness. They may even begin to use alliteration or rhyme. Remember whatever they suggest it is the start of their poem building. There is no such thing as a wrong poem and it doesn't have to rhyme!

Use different tunes and ask the children to give you their ideas. You will be surprised at how quickly they catch on to this idea.

## Creating poems as part of planned or intended learning

If a group of children are asked, 'What is a poem?' it is likely they will immediately respond by saying that it is something that rhymes or they might even use a rhyme. It is important for the adult to realise that creating poems is not an exercise in phonics and using rhyme. The previous chapter has highlighted the role of rhyme in helping children in the early stage of reading and again has highlighted that this should be an enjoyable and fun activity.

Creating poems with very young children is about encouraging them to use words and sounds in a slightly different way from their normal everyday speech patterns. In the following case study children were very definite that they needed to use rhyme until I explained that this was not always the case. After this they became more confident at using words in different ways.

---

### Creating poems in the nursery at St. Christopher's

Children had been searching for minibeasts and talking about them. They found a caterpillar and had been listening to the story of *The Hungry Caterpillar*.

I worked with two small groups in turn, five or six children in each and asked if they knew what a poem was. Some children said it was about things that rhymed. I explained that poems can rhyme but don't always have to rhyme and we were going to try to write our own poem using words that sounded right and told us something about the subject but didn't always have to rhyme.

#### Group 1

There was some discussion about which minibeast but they decided to choose a caterpillar. One child said he had found a frog in his garden and so we thought we could write about that too. We started the session with the children trying to move around like caterpillars. I then read two poems I had written about caterpillars (see anthology section, pages 137–8).

This led to the start of the poem which I scribed as they spoke.

> Wriggly wiggly like a worm
> Wriggly wiggly like a snake (*I asked the questions," 'What would he like to eat?' 'Did he have teeth like us?' This led to the choice of the word swallowing*)
> Swallowing leaves
> Crawling so fast
> Caterpillar food
> Leaves and leaves and leaves (*Children chose to repeat this word and felt a sense of rhythm as they said this line. I asked another question, 'What happens next to the caterpillar if he eats so many leaves?'*)
> Getting fat
> Spin your cocoon, sleep a while (*This phrase was suggested by a child and then they started to think of rhyming words: mile, pile, dial were listed.*)

---

Turn into a butterfly flap flap *(One child mimed the flap, flap as he said the words.)*
Make me smile

We then started to discuss how to write a poem about a frog.

Hop, hop was suggested and the group discussed how many hops they needed for the first line.

Some children were mentioning rhymes and pool and school came up. We had a discussion about frog school and what the frogs would learn. After this discussion children chose to use the phrase 'join your friends' rather than 'I like jumping'.

Hop hop hop hop hop
Join your friends in the pool
Hop hop hop all the way
Learn to play and jump in school

This poem is interesting as the last line seems to combine something of the children's own experiences of school and the frog. The internal rhyme of play and way is I think coincidental but adds to the poetic structure of this verse.

O. said, 'Frogs make tadpoles,' and came up with this nonsense verse:

Tadpoles froggy tadpoles
Tadpoles in your eyes eating pies.

## A spider poem by group 2

Spider crawls around
Crawling on the pavement
Silky circle web
Catch a green fly a blue fly a purple fly.

As we were talking about caterpillars one child said 'Why did the caterpillar crawl upon your head?'

I said that would make a lovely start to a poem and did they know any words that rhymed with head.

Children said bed, wed, red and so together we composed this poem. They needed some help with reversing word order so that the rhyming word came at the end of the line.

Why did the caterpillar crawl upon your head?
Looking for some leaves to munch leaves of green or red
Why did the caterpillar crawl upon your head?
Because he wanted to sleep in his cocoon bed
Why did the caterpillar crawl upon your head?
Changing into butterfly blue pink purple red.

Later in the garden I met two boys with magnifying glasses looking for minibeasts. They had an identification chart but told me they hadn't found any. They asked me which one I liked and we had a discussion about which they liked best. They chose a snail and I asked them if they knew any words which could describe a snail.

Snails live in jungles
Big shell on their back
They hide in their shell
Sliding slimy body

## Evaluation

The children were new to the idea of sitting down in a group to write a poem together and at the beginning many wanted to write their own poems about their own subject. They also wanted to draw pictures, but once we started discussing one particular subject they all joined in the general discussion and most children came up with a phrase that was used in the final poem. If there was a choice of word or phrase we listened to both and children decided which one to choose. It was mostly unanimous but occasionally we had to go with the majority vote.

In all cases, the children watched as I wrote down their words in shorter lines to fit in with poetic structure rather than long sentence structure. I re read the lines at each stage of the poem and it is surprising how a sense of rhythm emerges as the poem is read aloud. The children were very conscious that verses should rhyme and initially this inhibited them. However, after they had worked on a non rhyming poem I felt they were ready to try a rhyming verse and although they needed a bit more help they were very keen to do this and created the second caterpillar poem. The children were very proud of their efforts and thrilled when their teacher read them to the whole class later that morning.

## Planned learning experience based on special occasions

In the anthology there are several poems about bonfire night. Try reading some of these to the children around 5 November, then make the time to help them come up with their own poems. A simple starting point is to write down some of the children's sayings and then collate them into a poem. This can often have surprising results.

An example of planned poetry making is given below

| Day | Story/activity | Evaluation |
|---|---|---|
| | Learning intention: to develop subject specific vocabulary linked to bonfire fireworks | |
| | Letters and sounds: introduce onomatopoeic words – pop bang whoosh etc | |
| Wed 5 | Bonfire story *Whatever Next* and a selection of poems | Children listened well. Lots of discussion about bonfires and fireworks, talked about colours and sounds |
| Thurs 6 | Discussion about what they saw and heard use words to describe the sounds and what they saw. Adult to scribe to make the poem | Lots of excited discussions children needed reminding to listen to each other |
| Fri 7 | Re read the poem using large sheet. Give children copy of printed poem for them to decorate | Children talked about which part of the poem was theirs. Nathaniel kept saying pop bang crack pop bang crack as he worked |

The sentences were collated into the following poems, one by the morning group and another by the afternoon group.

### Fireworks

I saw fireworks
I heard bang at the park
Pshiss pshiss
Boom
I heard putt putt putt
I saw moon and stars
When I was in my bed
I heard FIREWORKS
and they went BANG
A BIG BANG BOOM BANG

### Fireworks

The fireworks go bang
The fireworks go
Wheeeeeee
The Fireworks go
Ooooooooooooooo
The noise sounds like
Jumping in muddy puddles
Pop pop pop
Lots of different colours
Little bits like colourful snow

At Christmas time children at Crosfield wrote the following poems.

### Christmas!

Christmas is tinsel we put it on the tree!
Christmas has a star on top of the tree!
Christmas has a bauble on the tree!
Santa gives us toys!
The cracker goes bang!
Christmas is baby Jesus asleep in the hay! Shh! Shh! Shh!

*(A poem by Savanna, Luke E, Penelope, Gabriella and Olivia)*

### Christmas!

Christmas is stars in the sky!
Christmas is funny with crackers!
Christmas has shooting stars!
Christmas has a lovely Christmas tree with funny things on it and acorns too!
Christmas has tinsel: lovely, pretty and shiny!
Father Christmas, Santa Claus, Saint Nicholas says 'ho,ho,ho!'
And he's coming to town!

*(A poem by James, Muhammad, Morgan, Elouise and Rosie)*

## Widening your repertoire and creating opportunities

Before children can create their own poems they need to have experienced a range of poetry. Hopefully they will have heard a wide range of nursery rhymes and songs from an early age. As I was writing this book I realised I had neglected to read poems to my grandchildren so now they have poems as well as bedtime stories. Lucy aged four loves looking through the Macmillan treasury of nursery rhymes and poems. There is an emotional bond and a physical one as she snuggles in close but she is listening intently to the sound patterns of the words as well as enjoying the illustrations. When she was only three we talked about poems and I asked her if she could make one. We looked at a rain stick that she enjoys using and as she was playing with it I asked her to tell me some words about it.

Noise like rain
Drop drop drop drop
Swoosh swoosh swoosh
Whoosh whoosh
Wish wish
Swish swish

By repeating the words she showed that she already seemed to have some under-standing of poetic form. The rhyme at the end seemed to just happen as she spoke and I scribed it as she was talking. There was some hesitation after the second line and I asked the question what sort of sound is it making and then she replied swoosh.

Niklas Pramling in his paper 'Introducing poetry making in early years educa-tion' writes in some detail about one of the challenges that faces young children. He gives an example (p. 385) of how children use the word 'like' as they are at this stage unable to use poetic similes. This is evident in three of the poems documented in this chapter. He writes how one child says 'The lizard is like a green lizard'. This is very similar to the chick poem where the children wrote 'What's a chicken? Well didn't you know they look like chickens'.

Pramling goes on to explain that one way of encouraging children to develop their poetic thinking is encourage them to tell 'how something appears and sounds to them, or maybe what it does'. When Lucy was making her rain stick poem, she was hesitant to begin with but when asked this sort of question came up with the onomatopoeic words 'whoosh' and 'swoosh', and was then able to put them into some sort of poetic order. The message for practitioners is to use the best practice approach of asking open ended questions and then maybe ask children to tell us a bit more. In nursery settings it is important to create a poetry friendly environment. This can be created not just by reading poems but occasionally printing them out so children can observe the different layouts of poems. The classroom rhyme book is a good way to share poems and children begin to understand the connections between the spoken and the written word. A short poem can be printed out in large type and displayed on the wall, perhaps with some illustrations.

Michael Rosen uses the term 'secret strings' to describe some of the complexities of what might make a poem. It is anything that links one word or phrase to another. Rhythm patterns, repeated words, rhymes, sounds, images or phrases and patterns of different kinds. Sometimes when sharing a poem it might be appropriate to listen to the words again and point out to the children some of these secret strings.

As they begin to create their poems the secret strings will be evident. Instead of asking children to just recount their trip to the farm this nursery teacher encour-aged them to collate their ideas and build a poem.

> One day we went to the farm
> On a coach we journeyed
> We talked to each other
> All the way to the farm
> Then we fed the cows
> 'I counted the bottles of milk'
> They were gentle
> The rabbits we stroked
> We saw pink pigs on the farm
> We went on the coach again
> Sleeping all the way.

Because she wrote out their ideas in this format and read it back to the children they were able to see the way it sat on the page. 'Rabbits we stroked' and 'on a coach we journeyed' are similar ways to use the verb. This is a secret string. 'Pink pigs' is an example of alliteration and the last four words, when read aloud slowly, give the poem a natural rhythmic ending.

## Using children's first hand experiences at home and nursery

Creating a poem with children is just a slightly different way of sharing the learning that is happening and extending the ways in which children think and feel. Hopefully it will enable them to become more confident about expressing themselves and using language with confidence. Poems can also be created at unexpected moments.

Rosie aged three has two older brothers and they all enjoy sharing poems and stories at home. They often play word games too and Rosie in has enjoyed books from a very early age. One morning as they were waiting to go to school, Mum said, 'Let's make a poem' and she offered an opening line. The children all added lines in turn and Rosie at three was able to join in imaginatively as they created this poem together.

> Down by the seaside
> The water is cold                    (Rosie)
> Children play in the sand
> Sea goes swishy swashy               (Rosie)
> Children surf
> Waves spatter and spit               (Rosie)
> Children chatter
> Having fun having fun FUN!

On the way home from nursery one wet day Rosie suddenly came out with the following:

> Splish splash splosh
> I love the rain tumbling on me
> Splish splash splee
> I don't like the rain tumbling on me.

What is interesting here is that she has adapted the last word to make it rhyme with me although when I asked her if she thought poems needed to rhyme she wasn't very sure.

While on holiday with our grandchildren, I talked about my ideas for this book and that night, Joshua aged seven, said he would like to write a poem. We had been on the beach many times that week and as he lay in bed he wrote the following:

**The crystal sea**

The deep blue sea shimmering in the sunset
From the horizon, waves so calm on the crystal clear sea.
As the sunlight fades we go to bed under the stars
Dreaming of playing in the sand

*(by Joshua T. Grahame)*

## Creating a poem in an appropriate space

The importance of making poetry friendly spaces is highlighted in Chapter 3. If creating poetry is to be given recognition in your setting, a good way to do this is by making a special poetry space.

If you have access to a stimulating outdoor environment try to use it. Look at the natural planting and add some rugs or cushions near some bushes under a tree or maybe in a wildlife area.

A small hideaway could be made in some bushes or some fabric and cushions under a tree will encourage children to sit still and maybe observe what is going on around them. If you have a corner you can add some fabrics or drapes to make a roof and place a few rhyme books inside.

Children will probably need an adult to scribe so it needs to be big enough for an adult to enter. In a reception class you could add some pens or pencils, notebooks or special pads for poetry writing. Paper could be headed with the words MY POEM just to make children more aware that this space can be used to write poems. Spaces can be made outdoors and indoors and if possible try to display some printed verses, rhyming and none rhyming. These can be printed out in fairly large type, perhaps illustrated to give some visual clues, laminated and placed either on the walls or made into a simple book.

The case study from Crosfield Nursery (below) about the blossom poems shows how the adults planned the activity and provided a space under the trees to give the children first hand experience as they created their poems together.

---

### Crosfield Nursery: 'Cherry blossom'

At Crosfield Nursery an annual highlight is the cherry blossom on the two large trees in the garden. In the book, *Outdoor Learning Through the Seasons* (2013), there is a description of the way in which the children used the blossom in their play and as an ingredient in their mud kitchen. They had produced art work about it, but to my knowledge no poems had been written. As they played with it today picking it up and throwing the petals one child said, 'It's like butterflies flying' and another said, 'It's like snow'.

This seemed to be a good starting point for these children to work in a small group to write a poem. A table and chairs was provided under the trees and

---

**FIGURE 5.2** Making a special place under the cherry tree allows children to get inspiration and first hand experience as they create their poem.

before the group of children began to think about the poem they spent some time lying down on the ground looking up through the trees.

They then listened to the lines of A. E. Housman's poem, 'The cherry tree' and another short poem in a book about the seasons. Mary, an early years educator at the nursery, asked the children to think about what they had said as they were playing. She wrote as they came up with their ideas. As the ideas were read back to them they were asked to make choices about which words sounded or fitted in best. 'Does it fall on the ground or fall on the floor?' Children agreed that floor sounded better as it began with the same letter as fall.

> Blossom blossom
> Awesome blossom
> Soft and falling
> Falling like rain falling like snow
> Flying like butterflies
> Throwing it in the air
> Up in the air
> It falls to the floor
> Blossoms are falling from the sky
> Until there is no more

The poem was printed out and children enjoyed illustrating their own copies. It was later printed in the newsletter for parents.

In this poem the grouping of words together and the repetition gives it structure and encouraged children to use language in a slightly different way. They were very pleased with the end result. The role of the adult needs to be supportive but it is important not to superimpose too many ideas. By giving children a choice of which word to use, you are giving them ownership of their poetry. Young children do not distinguish between the written and spoken word and it is important that the adult is able to scribe their ideas straight away lest they get forgotten in the flow of language. By rereading back these ideas to the children and asking some questions, children are helped to develop an awareness not only of the meaning of a word, but how it sounds and how it fits together with other words to make a sound pattern. Children will often create their own rhythmic patterns and I believe this sense of rhythm is either innate or comes from their earliest experiences of being rocked, held and soothed as a baby. It is essential that we continue to nurture this and allow it to develop.

## Creating different types of poems

Older children, particularly those in reception classes, may enjoy thinking about different ways to create poems. Talk to children about different types of poems and use examples before encouraging them to try to write their own.

### Shape poems

Children can draw their own shapes or use a template. A heart, a tree, or a snail are good ones to use. Anita Ganeri (2013), shows a poem written inside a raindrop shape just using words of the sounds of the raindrops. This is a very simple exercise and a good place to start.

Encouraging children to think about the sounds the words make is key. If children are working on alliteration as part of their literacy curriculum, writing poems is another good way to extend this learning.

### Kenning

These sound simple enough when read out loud, but it is often difficult for children to reverse the order of words to give the desired effect. The poetic form originated in Anglo Saxon and Norse poetry. In a kenning, an object is described in a two word phrase. The subject of the poem is not mentioned by name so the reader has to guess what it is. The poems are a form of riddle and children will love to hear them even if they find it difficult to write one. Examples can be found in *A First Puffin Book of Poetry*: page 22, 'Baby brother'; p. 27, 'My mum'; p. 65 'A friend'; p. 81, 'Who am I?' and 'What am I?' on p. 46.

### Haiku

The first haikus were written in Japan in the ninth century and are still very much part of their poetic culture today. A short poem, the first line contains five syllables, the second line has seven and the third line has five. Although they are short poems they are complete in themselves using sensory language to capture a feeling or image. They are often inspired by nature and could be an excellent way to incorporate literacy into the outdoor learning of your setting.

## Acrostic poems

These are poems composed using the first letter of each line to build up the name of the subject or title of the poem. Children will be able to do this using words from their existing vocabularies, and as they get better at it, they may be encouraged to use new words which they might hear in a discussion or in another poem read aloud by an adult. Examples of acrostic poems are seen in the anthology section in 'The seasons' 'Spring' 'Summer' and 'Autumn'.

## Writing a poem about a colour

There are several poems in the colour section in the anthology which can be read to children to give them some ideas. Once you are sure the children have an accurate knowledge of the colour spectrum it is an easy way to encourage discussion and creativity.

Ask children to close their eyes and ask if can see something pink and name or describe it. They may suggest pale roses, a tiny shell and pink ice cream or a lolly. Ask them to think of some words they might use with a lolly. Write down any words that the children suggest and say them to the children in different sequences and ask which they prefer.

Children in one group came up with

> Pinkety lick lickety pink
> Pink pink a strawberry drink

In connection with any work on letters and sounds (see previous chapter), you will probably be talking about onomatopoeic sounds with children as well as alliteration. Creating poems about bonfire night or weather poems, rain, wind and storms should offer good opportunities for children to express themselves and enjoy using words and creating word patterns.

## Creativity and poetry

Poetry is an expression of ideas and thoughts using words. It often describes things or paints pictures in our minds. Another way to encourage poetry writing with children at the end of Foundation Stage may be to use a different creative art form as inspiration. This could take the form of listening to a piece of music and asking children to write down or talk about ideas that come into their minds as they listen. 'The swan' from 'Carnival of the animals' by Saint Saens is a good one to start with. 'The planets' by Holst is powerful and dramatic, and 'Au clair de lune' by Debussy is soft and calming.

Looking at a painting can sometimes inspire children. 'Sunflowers' by Van Gogh is often used in schools and if children are encourage to look at this in detail they may come up with some surprising ideas. In many schools and settings children may recreate this through the media of paint but using language to create a poem about it is just as creative. Depictions of the seasons and the weather can be inspiring too.

## Conclusion

Effective early learning will only take place if adults understand the nature of children's play and the importance of exploration and discovery. Children need first hand experiences of the weather and the seasons. They need to sow and grow, to cook, to paint and draw. They need to be able to talk about these experiences and using poetry is often a way of supporting learning and also offering rich exciting language at the same time. Children need to base their first poems on practical knowledge and experience. By giving children a chance to create a poem we are demonstrating our respect for the child's creativity and language ability. The outcome is not as important as the process. Creating a poem is just another way of recording an experience. As children become more confident, an adult can help them to work with the words, to think about the order and the way they sound. In this way we are developing not only their language skills but also their thought processes. This will enable them to become thoughtful readers and hopefully to have the ability to interpret and discuss texts.

Children need to hear non rhyming poems and understand that a poem is different from a story. If they feel a poem has to rhyme this will limit their creativity. They need to be able to focus on the meaning of the words. A poem can express ideas in a more precise way than text and this may help children who are beginning to write for themselves. They will not be constrained by grammar and punctuation rules.

The most important requirement for young children to create poetry is an adult who is supportive and encouraging. Giving children the time and opportunity to create poems can be extremely rewarding. If the poem can be printed out children can share it with their peers and their families. This is 'writing for a purpose' but essentially fosters a sense of confidence and self esteem. Margaret Perkins, writing in *Teaching Poetry in the Early Years* (Lockwood, 2011) offers a case study where the children in a reception class are inspired by the teacher's own love of poetry. 'You don't teach poetry – you read poems, you give them a high profile. You expose children to rich language and let them play with it.'

## Useful additional resources

*I Can Write Poems* by Anita Ganeri 2013,Capstone Global Library Ltd.
This is a very useful book to have in a reception class as it is well illustrated and

good for children to look at. The print is large and will be accessible for early readers. Some children will need help with this. The helpful suggestions are directed towards the child and so with adult support this book could be a good starting point for more formal or planned poetry writing experiences. Includes clear explanations of acrostic poems, haiku, shape poems and free verse.

*It Doesn't Need to Rhyme Katie: Writing a Poem with Katie Woo* by Fran Manushkin illustrated by Tammie Lyon. Picture Window Books Capstone Publishing USA 2014.

A very useful book to share with a small group of children if you are thinking about creating some poems together. It will help to dispel some of children's ideas that poems need to rhyme and explore the idea that poetry can be a different way of expressing feelings and emotions.

## References

Pramling, N. (2009) 'Introducing Poetry Making in the Early Years', *European Early Childhood Education Research Journal*, Vol. 17, No. 3, 377-390.

Perkins, M. (2011) 'Teaching poetry in the early years', chapter 2 in Michael Lockwood (ed.) *Bringing Poetry Alive*, Sage Publications.

Watts, A. (2013) *Outdoor Learning Through the Seasons*. Routledge.

# Conclusion

Poetry is an integral and essential part of our existence as human beings. It is at the heart of our emotional being. It is used at times of great joy and great sadness. It is used to celebrate many special occasions and it can offer a new outlook on social problems as well as on the wonders of creation. Cultures across the world have their own strong traditions and we need to be aware of these as we work with diverse societies and children from many different ethnic backgrounds. Oral storytelling in verse began with the Greek myths. The Japanese have an age old tradition of haiku verse. Indian songs, black raps and folksongs from around the world all use poetry, both rhyming and non rhyming.

One of the most vital elements of poetry is the rhythm of the language used. This does not mean that is necessarily has to rhyme, but the way the words are put together often lends a sense of rhythm and poetic flow. A poem is arranged in a particular metre but in free verse it may be looser. Rhyme at the end of lines is the basis of many common forms. Rhyme did not enter European poetry until the middle ages. It may be arguable that not all rhyming verse is poetry. The most important factor is the quality of the language and the emotional powerfulness of the poem. It may succeed in making us laugh or cry, or touch on a whole range of other emotions. As we share poems with our children they may help us to recall something of our own childhood: a distant memory, a sight or a smell. By talking to children about your memories you are establishing an emotional connection as well as possibly offering something of an earlier way of life. The book began by examining the way in which poetry has been used from the earliest of times through to the present day. Human beings from many backgrounds and diverse cultures recognise that poetry can play an important part in their lives.. We need to ensure therefore that we offer it to our children from birth and throughout their time in nursery. Researchers are becoming more and more aware of the way in which the brain develops from conception and the importance of singing to a baby even before it is born. If babies hear songs and lullabies on a regular basis, they will respond readily to the rhythm patterns they hear in spoken verse. This in turn develops the skills of listening and by six weeks old babies are becoming attuned to the sounds of the specific language or languages they hear most.

There are many ways in which poetry can be interwoven into the early years curriculum. We are required to offer a rich language environment for children. There is little guidance however on what this entails, but if we do not offer poetry we are depriving children of a rich source of language and creative expression. It should be part of the planned learning of a nursery setting but it may occur spontaneously both there and in the home. Adults may suddenly recall and recite a childhood verse of nursery rhyme. Children may suddenly enrich and accompany their own play by making up a chant or song. They may repeat or invent words, play with words and sounds or recite or chant lines from a poem, a story or a song.

One of the most important roles of the adult, be it parent or practitioner, is to introduce a wide variety of poetry to children from birth onwards. Singing lullabies and traditional rhymes is a good starting point and offers emotional security right from the start. This can be continued through a shared love of language, the sounds, patterns and rhythms as you sing, recite or read to your child. Poems can be shared at all sorts of different times. They can be part of nappy changing, tidying up and story time, meal times or just quiet time, sharing a book of verse. As children begin to understand the meanings of the words, there are many poems and rhymes which will encourage skills of listening and concentration. Counting rhymes, action rhymes and finger rhymes all have a valuable part to play in children's learning across the curriculum. Poems which relate to children's everyday experience should be introduced and then, as children become more competent users of language they can understand poems that express different emotions. Funny poems and nonsense poems both contribute to the sense of enjoyment that comes from sharing poetry.

The fundamental purpose of sharing poetry with children is to offer a rich language experience which should be enjoyed by both adults and children. There are however additional dramatic benefits as this has been shown to have a direct bearing on children's early reading skills. If children hear rhyme from an early age, they can discriminate more easily as they hear rhyming sounds and this helps them to make the links between the sounds they hear and the marks on the page. Poems, verses and rhyming stories can be used with good effect to help children develop these skills.

Children need to hear poems before they can create them. They will respond to the rhythm patterns and the way the words hang together. If they have heard a wide variety of rhyming and non rhyming poems they may find it easier to create their own word pictures.

When helping children to create their own poems it is important not to focus on rhyme but to help children to use words in different ways. Talk with children to develop their ideas, if children cannot write for themselves jot down their ideas and then discuss alternative forms of expression. Children learn to make judgements about language. They listen to the sounds and the effects of using words in different sequences. They learn to ask questions about words and language. They may not always understand something but are developing enquiring minds.

Through helping children create their own poems, we are not only supporting the development of the basic skills of literacy, but hopefully we can inspire enthusiasm and confidence in their own ability to use words creatively. It is important that they can understand that there is no need to focus on just rhyming. This often inhibits rather than promotes language. They need to be able to enjoy the freedom that a poem can offer. It enables emergent writers to use and make sense of words in an economical way and not to be overly concerned with the narrow rules of grammar and punctuation which can so often impede the creative flow of a young writer. Sensitive intervention by adults is needed to scribe when necessary and then to encourage older children to write for themselves.

Sharing your life with very young children can be exhausting and frustrating at times but there can be many special spontaneous moments that often open our eyes to the world in which we live. Seeing the world through the eyes of a small child can be a magical experience. It may be shuffling through autumn leaves, watching a train go by, looking closely at a worm or a raindrop. Often these moments awaken some reminiscence of our own childhood. If we are able to enter the child's world we are better equipped to understand how children learn and how we can support, engage and extend their learning. Poetry can be a valuable tool in this process. A short poem shared at the right moment can reinforce and extend learning. Rhythms and rhymes will engage the youngest of children and they will often be able to listen and join in with a short poem or verse. A poem that is relevant to the child's own experience may present an idea in a slightly different way. It may introduce new vocabulary but the rhythm will help children to listen and to retain the language. Children with English as an additional language may respond to a poem as the short lines are easier for them to grasp and decode. Adults need to build up their own repertoire of easily accessible poetry and it is for this reason that I have written so many poems relating to children's everyday experiences particularly those that happen in the outdoor environment. Recent emphasis has been given to the importance of the natural world and the way it can influence children's wellbeing and learning. The outdoor spaces we can offer to children have a great impact on the nature of their learning. Careful and imaginative planning will ensure we make the most of every corner and every opportunity to enable children to interact with the natural world. It will also enable children to access books and poetry at all times both inside and outdoors.

Children should be encouraged to learn some poems by heart; this helps to develop memory skills. As they become confident readers they should be encouraged to read poetry as well as fiction. This will ensure they have the love of poetry which may well stay with them through life. It may help them to deal with emotional turmoil or enhance a sense of peace or a scene of beauty. Robert Fisher (2000, p. 8) said

> *Poetry may do many things, helps children to see to hear and to feel, to understand themselves and others better, to help them grow as people and to develop their understanding of words as tools for thinking.*

A poem encourages pictures in the mind. Children's attention is often held at story time by bright illustrations and they learn to tell the story through the pictures rather than the words. A poem encourages children to listen and focus on the meaning of the words. Children need to have the experience of forming mental images from what they hear if they are to make the connections they need to be able to read and write. Games or songs heard on the computer or television predetermine what the child sees and bypass this important neurological step.

Children may need to question or discuss the meanings of words or parts of a poem with an adult and other children and this in itself promotes an enquiring attitude and disposition. Children will soon be able to develop pictures in their minds, an essential component of a good imagination. It takes time to absorb a poem, the sounds, the pictures and sometimes even the smells that it evokes, as well as the story it conveys. In Fisher 2000, he writes (p.2).

> *A poem can transform the ordinary into the extraordinary. It can give voice to an inner world of dreams and imaginings.*

Through talking to adults involved in this book I have discovered that many of them have enjoyed poetry themselves but have not used it very much in their settings. Hopefully this book will inspire parents and practitioners to obtain some of the anthologies and use them on a daily basis.

The very first lines of this book stated that poetry predated literacy and it is important that we bear this in mind. Oral literacy, that is speaking and listening, is an essential part of our children's lives from the moment they are born. We need to emulate this tradition of offering poetry before children are able to write. They need to hear and feel it. They need to absorb it into their being and hopefully it will give them a resource which they can use in later life. It may serve to help them get through a serious illness or the death of someone dear. It can enhance moments of happiness and add new, exciting dimensions to something familiar.

Poetry is an art form in its own right but it is very often linked with music and drama or painting and drawing. Poetry plays an important role in the creative language experiences we offer to our children. It will develop not only their language skills but their imagination. It will lead them into a world of colour, sound and feeling. It is bound up with music and song and children may respond in many different ways. Children learn to express themselves in so many ways. Poetry needs to be a part of our lives to such an extent that children absorb and hear it without separating it in their minds from the other creative forms of expression and language. It needs to be something that is built into their daily life.

Loris Malaguzzi the founder of the Reggio Emilia preschools wrote a poem 'The hundred languages of children' in recognition of the multitude of ways in which children can express their ideas, thoughts, feelings or frustrations. For him, the essential creative nature of the child cannot be separated into parts and the schools and cultures only serve to take away some of this essential creative expression.

The possibilities for the 'languages' are endless – dancing, dreaming, playing, questioning, singing, reasoning, imagining, listening, laughing, crying, loving, hating, painting, sculpting, exploring, experimenting.

## The hundred languages of children

No way. The hundred is there.
The child
is made of one hundred.
The child has
a hundred languages
a hundred hands
a hundred thoughts
a hundred ways of thinking
of playing, of speaking.

A hundred always a hundred
ways of listening
of marvelling, of loving
a hundred joys
for singing and understanding
a hundred worlds
to discover
a hundred worlds
to invent
a hundred worlds
to dream.

The child has
a hundred languages
(and a hundred hundred hundred more)
but they steal ninety-nine.
The school and the culture
separate the head from the body.
They tell the child:
to think without hands
to do without head
to listen and not to speak
to understand without joy
to love and to marvel
only at Easter and at Christmas.

They tell the child:
to discover the world already there
and of the hundred
they steal ninety-nine.

They tell the child:
that work and play
reality and fantasy

science and imagination
sky and earth
reason and dream
are things
that do not belong together.

And thus they tell the child
that the hundred is not there.
The child says:
No way. The hundred is there.

*(Loris Malaguzzi, translated by Lella Gandini)*

**Let us not be guilty of stealing the ninety-nine. Let us offer as much as we can through the tradition of poetry. Link it with music, with sculpture, painting, drawing, dance, drama and song but do not ignore it. It needs to be an essential part of early learning for every child.**

## References

Fisher, R. (2000) *First Poems for Thinking*. Oxford: Nash Pollock Publishing.

Malaguzzi, L. (2011) 'The hundred languages of children', In C. Edwards, L. Gandini and G. Forman (eds) *The Hundred Languages of Children.* Praeger.

# Poetry anthology for children in their early years

## Anthology contents

The poems in most sections of this anthology are arranged so that the poems suitable for younger children appear at the beginning of each section. However many poems can be used across a wide variety of ages and suitability may be defined by the language abilities of children rather than chronological age. Children can enjoy poems just for the sound patterns and the rhythms of the language even if they don't necessarily understand much of the meaning.

In the section The garden, poems are arranged in seasonal order starting with poems appropriate for January and then moving through the gardening year. In the sections Garden creatures, Pets and Colours, the poems are arranged in categories rather than age appropriateness.

# Spring

### Spring is best

A crocus is peeping through the earth
A bird is cheeping in the nest
Animals are giving birth
Of all the seasons **SPRING** is best

### Five yellow daffodils

*Resources:* 5 daffodils, real if possible otherwise artificial ones could be used.
*Activity*: encourage children in close observation of the flower, its petals and trumpet. Drawing or painting the flowers. Different media could be water colours, chalks or pastels.

Five yellow daffodils
Straight and tall
Growing in the garden
Over by the wall

Along came … *Insert child's name*
Looking so cool
Picked a yellow daffodil
And took it off to school.

Four yellow daffodils etc then Three Two One

### Yellow in spring

A gleam of yellow in the spring
A primrose peeping or a bluetit's wing
Sweet fluffy chickens scratching the ground
Long dangling catkins dancing around

### Catkins

*This poem can be read to children and they can be encouraged to substitute different words to describe firstly the catkins then the birds. Then they can choose another spring time subject and use a similar format to make up their own poems.*
*A Japanese haiku only consists of thirteen syllables so short can be beautiful and often profound.*

Catkins
Yellow pollen tails
Rippling and curling

Birds
Dart and swerve
Searching sheltered spots for nests

### Spring flowers

Winter days are nearly gone
And spring is in the air
Birds are nesting in the trees
And there are flowers everywhere

Tulips open pink and red
Purple crocus by the wall
Blossom heavy on the boughs
Bright yellow daffodils so tall

Snowdrops now have nearly gone
But look amongst the leaves so green
Pale primroses are peeping out
And purple violets can be seen

### Early spring

Pink blossom heavy
Against a pale blue sky

While green buds unfold
Even though it's cold
The flowers are there
A sight full of promise
Spring is in the air

### Green in spring

Green speckled skin
On a golden eyed frog
Emerald green moss
On a dark damp log

Green buds uncurling
Green shoots unfurling
New leaves are growing
And the grass needs mowing!

### Senses in springtime

*This poem was written with a group of four- and five-year-olds. We discussed the five senses and the first line of each verse was given to them and using a computer the adult wrote the ideas as they were agreed. You could either read this out to your group or try it and see what they come up with for themselves.*

When I go out I touch the spring
Soft fluffy chicks, velvety buds
Sticky furry chestnut buds
Smooth new leaves

When I go out I see the spring
Bright sun on bright green leaves
Yellow daffodils, dancing in the wind
Wriggling tadpoles in the pond

When I go out I hear the spring
Blackbirds and robins chirrup and sing
Bleating of newborn lambs
Tiny cheep of baby chicks

When I go out I taste the spring
Fresh clear water but at Easter time
The velvety taste of the chocolate egg
And for tea yummy eggy soldiers

When I go out I smell the spring
Damp soil and bluebell waves
Cherry blossom and the first cut of the grass

### New growth in springtime

Flowers and grass are quickly growing
Gardeners busy, neighbours mowing
Buds are swelling, leaves unfurling
New born baby, toes uncurling,
Turns to watch the fresh green leaves
Gently waving in a warm spring breeze

### Sights and sounds in spring

Catkins dangle in the breeze
Buds are swelling on all the trees
Tiny flowers push through the ground
And birdsong makes a joyful sound

### Spring flower

One day
  A bud
    Shows
       Sepals shrink
      A flower
        Grows
          Opens wide
         Petals pure
First
  Just
    One
      Then several
      More
        Carpet like
       Spring
         Flower
        Floor

## Spring waking

Awakening
Rising
Sap in a leaf
Buds swell
Unfurling uncurling
Gossamer green
Against a grey cold cloud sky
And then the blue
Bright light blue
Leaves uncurl to greet the
Warm spring sun


## The primrose

Pale yellow peeping
Shyly, not knowing whether to
Emerge,
Or wait another day
A pale weak sun,
The decision made
A bud unfolds
Perfection of shape
Resting in folds
Of wrinkly green


## Spring (an acrostic poem)

Suddenly its spring again
Prancing lambs on sunny hills
Raindrops glisten on daffodils
Ice has melted, snow has gone
New buds burst, birds in song
Glorious notes in sweet refrain

# Summer

### Ice cream

*This poem can be used with very young children. Shout out the first two lines loudly and then read the next line in a slow heavy voice emphasising the rhythms*

Ice creams for sale
Ice creams for sale
A pink one, a mint one, or a chocolate chip bar
Lick it very carefully or it won't go far

*Ask children to pretend they are licking an ice cream and use these words as they do so: dripping, licking, tongue flicking, ice cream melting.*

### Down to the beach

Down to the beach down to the sea
Build a big sandcastle just for me

Down to the beach down to the sea
Splash in the waves and jump for glee

Down to the beach down to the sea
Play on the sand and back home for tea

**The beach bag**

*When introducing this poem to very young children or those with EAL try to have a beach bag with the items inside it. These visual clues will help them to understand the poem. It can also be read again as children do the actions.*

Pick up the bag – carry with care
Down the steps we're nearly there
Put the bag down and open it wide
Put in your hand and find something inside
Here is a bucket fill it with sand
Pat it down carefully with the palm of your hand

Here is a spade shiny and new
I can dig in the sand and so can you
We can make a castle or dig a deep hole
A sand car, a dinosaur or even a mole

Here is the sun cream, it's kept out of reach
But we always use it when out on the beach
Rub on your arms your legs and your nose
Your tummy, your feet and even your toes
Rub it in well on everyone
To keep us all safe from the heat of the sun

Now what is this still to get out
A very large towel – lets open it out
My feet are sandy cold and wet
The towel's warm and furry – just perfect

**A day by the sea**

Buckets, spades, towels and mats
Sandwiches, drinks, sun cream and hats
We carry them down onto the beach
And find a place where the tide cannot reach

Spread out the mats and take off our clothes
Lots of sun cream, especially my nose
I run in the sand and then want to dig
I've made a sandcastle it's not very big

It's time for a swim, run down to the sea
Jump through the waves as they break over me

The water's quite cold I really don't care
I might even lie down in it, do you think I dare?

Waves are sparkling and children have fun
Some have small boats and others have none
But whatever we do we surely agree
There's nothing as good as a day by the sea!

## Summertime

*This poem could be used with children from three depending on their language abilities. If you feel it's too long just use one or two verses to begin with and then as children become familiar with these add some more. There are a lot of points for discussion as the poem relates different aspects of the summer.*

Summertime, summertime, days are cool
Why can't we use our paddling pool?
It's started to rain and the wind is blowing
It's cold and I think it could almost be snowing

Summer summertime at last some sun
We'll go outside and have some fun
Build a den and climb a tree
Perhaps we could plan a trip to the sea

Summertime, summertime, at last it's hot
Cream and sunhats and a shady spot
A trip to the beach or a trip to the park
When bedtime comes, it's not even dark

Summertime, summertime, long lazy days
Strawberries tomatoes sweet corn and maize
Bright summer flowers buzzing with bees
More insects hiding where nobody sees

Summer time, summer time, it's almost past
Days on the beach, I wish it would last
But autumn is coming and the weather is cool
Holidays over and back to school

## Butterfly

Butterfly butterfly, what will you do
Settle on flowers yellow or blue

Dip your tongue in nectar sweet
Then flutter away in the summer's heat

## Going to the beach

Is this the road down to the beach?
I can see the sea almost in reach
Park the car and unpack all our stuff
There's lots of bags so we hope it's enough

There's buckets and spades, balls and a bat
Sun cream, towels and everyone's hat
Extra jumpers in case it gets cold
And as much food and drink as the rucksack will hold

Lock up the car and off we trot
The sun's coming out and it's getting quite hot
First thing to do is spread out the mat
Get changed, find the suncream and put on my hat

Then at last we can run down to the sea
Waves are sparkling as we jump in with glee
It still feels quite cold but I need to swim
Armbands blown up and at last I am in!

## Sun protection

We need to think about the weather
Before we go outside today
The sun is shining and it's hot
I just want to get outside to play

'Wait a moment, just stand there,
Sun cream first' says my mummy
She puts the cream on arms and legs
She even rubs it on my tummy

## Daybreak

Sunlight streams
Through my window
How can I sleep?
A new day is dawning

Singing birds
Invite me out
Into the garden
They don't know its
Only five o clock
In the morning!

## Sea treasure

Each wave brings us treasures from afar
A tiny pebble, fish shaped like a star
Another will hurl a large piece of wood
An old piece of net, a child's torn hood
Another reveals an old plastic crate
A large grey stone, the head of a skate.
Now here is a seed from a far off land
Lying forgotten on a deserted strand

## On the beach (A sensory poem)

I touch
    The rocks
        Cold, wet smooth
            yet jagged
                Barnacles
                    Limpets dry and rough
I smell
    Seaweed
        Salty strong smell of the sea
            The salt spray on the breeze
I taste
    Sun cream,
        Salt on my lips
            And the sweet cold of summer
                Strawberry ice cream
I hear
    Seagulls mewling
        Children shouting
            Waves lapping
                Curling over the stones

I see
    Sea sky blue
        Clouds scurrying
            Dogs hurrying
                White foam spraying
                    Children playing
                        The day stretching out along the shore

## Summer in the city

The heat is rising through the dust,
The sun beats down on the pavements hot
A cat stretched and strolls as if it must
Seek shelter – find a cooler spot

The cars race by, untouched by heat
A shimmering sea of tar and smells
The road is sticky to my feet
Where is the sea, the sand, the shells?

## The rock pool

A world enclosed
By granite
Laced with seaweed
A place where
I gaze
For hours
Tiny shells
Anemones
A crab
And then
The shrimp

In goes the net
Slowly
He meets it
Curious,
He moves forward
I quickly lunge
But raise
An empty net.

### The sea

*This prose poem could be read to older children particularly those who will have experienced the beach. Children could describe their own experiences and then think about some special words they could use.*

'Ripples of silver, small specks, a white sea bird, flash of black swooping low as cormorant flies purposefully westwards.

Gentle ripples, waves unfurl over sandy beach, lapping on a wide sandy shore curling over stray shells of pink, razor sharp blades, and curved pebbles worn by time.'

### Summer (an acrostic poem)

*Children in reception classes or KS 1 will enjoy seeing the use of initial letters at the beginning of each line. Some may be able to use this idea in their own writing. If they are able to do this then forget the rhymes at this stage and concentrate on the beginning word for each line.*

Sun is blazing from the bright blue sky
Umbrellas stripy and grand
Men are swimming in the sea
Mother's asleep on the sand
Everyone is having fun
Raindrops starting – quick let's run

# Autumn

**Conkers**

*This is a finger rhyme and children need to make appropriate actions. Large arms for the tree, small fists for the conkers and a basket shape using both hands. If you have a display with conkers in it, laminate the poem and maybe illustrate it with some photographs or drawings and put it above the display.*

Here is the tree with leaves so brown
Here are the conkers about to fall down
Be very careful, they're starting to fall
Here is a basket to gather them all.

**Leaves in autumn**

*This can be used with children from three onwards. Read the poem twice and then ask if anyone knows what **swirling twirling** etc means. Can children demonstrate with body movements? Then do the same with the words **furling** and **curling**. Once the children know the meaning of the words, they can mime or dance as they pretend to be the leaves.*

Leaves
Leaves swirling
Leaves twirling
Leaves fall to the ground

## Autumn colours

*Use this poem after children have observed the changing colours of leaves for them-
selves. There may be some new colour words for them to hear, e.g. ruby. You may
need to explain that the trees are not literally burning but the colours are the colours
of the flames. The word 'burn' can be used to describe colours too. Why are the shadows getting longer? This might link up with the shadow poem in the weather section.*

Leaves changing
Green to orange
Red and gold
Dry and crisp

Trees burn
Flame colours
Orange, amber
Gold and ruby

Sunlight glints
And shadows
Lie long
In the wet grass

## Trees at Knaphill

Twiggy black fingers reaching out
Dotted with gold
Pale gold suspended in autumn mists
Fairy gold shimmering in bright sun
Bronze gold heavy in autumn rain
All waiting for a winter storm

## Autumn in the country

Apples are heavy and hang from the tree
Underneath I wait patiently
To catch a juicy one as it falls
Usual shouts of, 'It's time for bed'
Must I go in yet? The sky is all red
Now off to bed, as still Mum calls

## Autumn harvest

Autumn winds blow strong and chill
Unruly leaves are fluttering nigh
The farmer gathers the last of the corn
Under the roof, the stack is high
Mellow fruits hang heavy and low
New seeds are forming just waiting to grow.

## Autumn in the garden

The sun is shining brightly
The leaves are turning red
Can we play outside today?
Wellies on, the teacher said.

Wellies on what does she mean?
The sun is out, the sky is blue
But the grass is soaking wet
Not from the rain, but from the dew

Each leaf and blade is sparkling bright
Dew comes down at dead of night
Diamonds shining fresh and clean
Dew drops on a bed of green

## Autumn in the town

Summer has gone and it's autumn again
Off to school in the cold wet rain
But the sun comes out and puddles shine
Webs glisten with threads silvery fine

We scrunch in the leaves beneath our feet
Find sweet chestnuts to roast and eat
Time for a short play in the park
Sky glowing red before it gets dark

## Autumn is here

The leaves have turned
To shades of gold
The weather's beginning
To feel quite cold

Blackberries hang
Shiny and dark
Conkers fall down
From the tree in the park

Autumn is here
And I scrunch through the leaves
As they carpet the pavements
Under the trees

**Autumn winds**

*Read the poem on its own first then maybe re read it and ask the children to make the sounds of the wind either at the end of the lines or the end of the verses (This links with Aspect 6: Voice sounds, in Letters and Sounds (DfES 2007, see References, Chapter 4)*

Wind is blowing
Rushing sound
Leaves are falling
To the ground

Wind is roaring
Whooshing sound
Leaves are whirling
Round and round

Wind is whistling
A very strong breeze
But no leaves are left
Hanging on trees

Wind is whispering
A scuffling sound
Stamping and scrunching
Through leaves on the ground.

**Five senses in autumn**

*This is a non rhyming poem and children should be encouraged to listen to the words carefully and talk about their own experiences. The poem could form the basis of a class lesson for older children as they discuss the five senses and maybe write their own poems. The poem can also be used with younger children and maybe could link in with a collection of fruits, chestnuts, conkers and autumn leaves for children to explore for themselves.*

When I go out, I smell autumn
The dampness of grass and leaves
Ripe fruit, fungus and
Bitter wood smoke in the air

When I go out, I taste autumn
Juicy pears, crisp apples
Chestnuts sweet
And ripe dark plums

When I go out, I feel autumn
Sharp green spikes hide
Smooth conkers and the
Mist is damp on my hair

When I go out, I hear autumn
Leaves crunching
High winds in the trees
And twittering of migrating birds

When I go out, I see autumn
Shiny dewdrops on a web
Fire touched sunsets and leaves
A blaze of orange yellow and red

# Winter

**Ice and snow**

Ice and snow ice and snow
Be very careful how you go
Snow and ice snow and ice
Sliding round is rather nice

**The five senses on a winter's night**

*Another sensory poem to be used in connection with children's learning and growing
understanding of the senses. If you can take the children outside in the dark try to
note what they observe with their senses and use this to make up their own verses –
they don't have to rhyme!*

What can you see on a dark winter's night?
A thin crescent moon and stars twinkling bright

What can you hear on a dark winter's night?
Fireworks crackling and whooshing, red, gold and white

What can you touch on a dark winter's night?
A swirl of white snowflakes, feathery light

What can you smell on a dark winter's night?
The smoke of a bonfire as it curls out of sight.

What can you taste on a dark winter's night
Satsumas, hot chocolate a fireside delight

## A grey day in winter

We run outside
And look at the sky
At the moment it's cloudy
But still quite dry

The grey clouds hang
Heavy over our school
It's not very warm
In fact it's quite cool

We run to keep warm
And shout as we play
We can still go outside
Even though it's so grey.

## Winter cold

Why is the wind so cold today?
Do you think snow is on the way?
I'm wearing my gloves and a nice woolly hat
But my feet are frozen. Why is that?

I need to jump and run around
It's harder to move on frozen ground
I'll clap my hands and stamp my feet
And this will give my body heat.

## Cold in winter

Winter frost sparkles on rock hard ground
Icicles melt with a tinkling sound
Numb fingers struggle to tie my shoe
Teeth are chattering, lips are blue.

Time to go home and warm up my toes
Shake my fingers and blow my nose
A nice hot drink is waiting for me
It's not very long, then it's time for tea.

**Playing out in winter**

It's really cold outside today
But please can I go outside to play
I'll wear my gloves and my new red hat
My wellies are there next to the mat

I'll put them on all by myself
I've got a new scarf high up on the shelf
I'll keep warm by running round and round
And I'll be very careful, there's frost on the ground

The grass is covered in layers of white
The frost makes the garden a beautiful sight
My feet make dark marks and so does my ball
When it bounces off the frosty wall

I'll splash in the puddles – that will be nice
Oh no, I forgot, they've all turned to ice
But then I can slip and slither and slide
As over the ice I carefully glide

**Out in the snow**

My wellies are on and I'm ready to go
Outside in the garden to play in the snow
I open the door, what a glorious sight,
Trees, paths and bushes all covered in white.

What shall I do and where shall I go?
I can't quite decide what to do in the snow
I might build a snowman and give him black eyes
Or make lots of snowballs to throw and surprise

I know what I'll do; I'll lie on the ground
I'll make a snow angel as my arms move around
If I pull at this branch on the very tall tree
I can make a new snow shower fall down over me.

I'll jump and I'll run and I'll walk in the snow
I make different foot marks wherever I go
There aren't many tracks on this blanket of white
It's glittering and sparkling – a magical sight

### Senses in the snow

*Before reading this to the children talk through what we mean by the five senses. Ask them what they enjoyed looking at in the snow. Have they tasted the snow? Touched it? Older children might enjoy making up their own poems based on their personal experiences. Remember a poem does not have to rhyme!*

Red wellies
Bright
On sparkling white
Crunch – a soft sound
As we tread the ground

Blue gloves
Off
To touch and feel
Soft cold
White gold

Long scarf
Unwound
Tongue out
Fresh smooth ice
Tasting – nice

Eyes uncovered
Dazzled
And falling flakes
White tracery of snow
On black branch
In floating dance

Noses
Cold and pink
Glowing in the sharp
Sting of snow fresh air
And snow flaked hair

### Winter time

It really takes a lot of time
Getting ready to go out
I've found my hat and got my coat
'Where's my gloves?' I loudly shout.

'They're over here' my mum replies
'You left them near the door,
Put on your wellies now, and please
Don't get mud on my clean floor!'

At last we're done and wrapped up warm
We run along towards the park
Just time to swing and climb and play
Before the sun sets and it gets dark

**Snow**

When I got out of bed this morning
I couldn't believe my eyes
It had snowed in the night
The ground was all white
This was a special surprise

When I put on my clothes this morning
I dressed to go out in the snow
Red gloves, hat and coat
A scarf round my throat
Wellies and socks to make my feet glow

When I went out to play this morning
I gathered and scooped up the snow
I made a big ball
And hit next door's wall
White crystals flew out high and low.

When I met all my friends this morning
A snowman just had to be made
A bright carroty nose
Stick arms and toes
And a body built with a spade.

**Snowflakes**

Grey sky unfurling
Snowflakes twirling
Snowflakes swirling
Whirling down

Snowflakes floating
Gently floating
White blanket
Covers town

## A snowflake

*A poem to use with older children. If they want to discuss it that's fine but not always necessary. A poem can be enjoyed just for its own sake without the need for dissection as often happens in key stage 1 and 2 classrooms.*

White,
Pure and still
A snowflake
Perfection of pattern
Symmetry and beauty
Only preserved for moments
Before becoming
A lost face in the crowd

## Snowstorm

*A poem to use with older children, perhaps in a reception class.*

The sky is heavy and dark
Threateningly full
But the world is still
The countryside
Holding its breath
Waiting
Expectant
Fearful
Yet unexpectedly it happens
Silently
Stealthily
A few flakes gently drifting
Stopping
Almost wanting to return to the clouds
Lonely
Waiting for others
Then suddenly
Swirling drifting dancing
The grey has opened to reveal
A miracle of white feather light flakes

Reluctant to land
Nudging each other
For a place to
Settle
The world is magic now
Trees are heavy and still
Each branch each twig defined
A tracery of unknown beauty
Against the sky
So clearly outlined
Is this the same garden we knew?
Only yesterday
Bleak and bare
Transformed into paradise

## Icicles

Shimmering
Translucent
Penetrating space
They hang
Suspended
Droplets
Frozen into
Pencil point
I reach out
Crack and snap
Then taste
The slippery coldness
Smoothing my tongue

## Winter world

Tree fingers
   Stretch across the sky
      Leaves still hang
         Persistent
           Clinging to the tree
           Unable to live
            Unable to die
           Until the wind
          Takes pity
           Swirling
            Whirling
             Releases their hold

## The weather

*The majority of poems about snow, frost and ice are in the winter section above. There is poem about thunder in the section on rhyme, rhythm and alliteration*

**Our weather!**

*This poem can be used as a basis for discussion about making the choice of suitable clothing according to the weather of the day. Looking out of the window is a good way to start the discussion.*

What will the weather be like today?
I need to go out with my friends and play
What shall I wear, my coat and hat
Sandals or shorts or wellies and mac?

Look out of the window
Look at the sky
The sun is shining and the clouds are high
I need my sandals and maybe my shorts
A wide sunhat and sun cream of course

Look out of the window
Look at the sky
The clouds are racing way up high
It's windy and cold, a hat and a coat
A warm woolly scarf around my throat

Look out of the window
Look at the sky
Dark grey clouds fill the sky
Waterproof trousers, a waterproof top
Wellies are needed as the rain won't stop

## Shadow poem

My shadow is my special friend
He loves to play with me
On sunny days he's by my side
Lying on the ground
But when the skies are dark and grey
He's nowhere to be found
It's when the sun is shining high
He's lying on the ground

## Playing with shadows

Look *MUM* I'm standing on your head (*use any suitable name of adults after 'Look'*)
And now I'm jumping on your arm
I can hop along your legs
But you won't come to any harm

I'm playing with YOUR SHADOW (*children shout out the last two words*)

## Sea mist

Grey sea mist rolling up the street
Curling round the houses
Swallowing the trees
Hiding all till afternoon
When helped by the salty breeze
It clears and seagulls shriek once more
White against the blue

## Poems about rain

### Puddles puddles everywhere (An action rhyme)

*Read this to the children first so they hear it and know what to expect. Place a slow emphasis on the words run, jump and splash.*

*Then ask them to stand up and move appropriately to the words. Look around to see the puddle, take a short run and then a jump. Then test with one leg and wobble in the mud! This can be used outside with real puddles or back inside to pretend, after children have been splashing outside.*

Puddles, puddles everywhere
Run jump splash
Here's a big one could be deep
Test it first, maybe creep
Try your toe – it's not too sticky
A puddle of mud can be quite tricky
Puddles, puddles everywhere
Run jump splash!

### Playing in the rain

*A poem suitable for children aged two to five. Before reading it talk about why they need to wear suitable clothing. What would this be? Can they dress themselves? Possible new vocabulary to be discussed – flood, deluge.*

It's raining, it's raining, it's raining today
And I really want to go out to play
But I can go out if I wear the right clothes
And I don't mind the raindrops tickling my nose

Wellies, a splash suit or a coat with a hood
Waterproof trousers, they're really good.
Getting them on is a bit of a struggle
But then I can search for a really large puddle

Now I am out and splashing around
Raindrops are making a pattering sound
The grass is so wet it's turning to mud
And the pools in the garden are making a flood

I need to make boats – maybe some leaves
There are some big ones just there under the trees
Some grass or a stick to push them around
They float gently along without making a sound

Wearing my waterproofs I kept warm and dry
In spite of the deluge falling out of the sky
I made marks in the mud, and stirred it around
And splashed in the puddles on the soggy wet ground

## April showers

I've planted my seeds and they've started to grow
Lettuces beans and sweet peas for flowers
They need lots of sun and also some rain
The best things for them are warm April showers.

## Grey clouds

Grey clouds heavy in the sky
Its looks like rain is on the way
The sky is heavy
Purple and grey
It's going to be
Another wet day

## Rain

*These three short poems should be read slowly and deliberately giving a heavy accent to each syllable so children pick up the rhythms and hear the rhyming patterns.*

Rain lashing
Cars splashing
Thunder crashing
Lightning flashing

Raindrops patter
Raindrops splatter
Feet go splash
Feet go splosh
Splash splosh splash splosh SPLASH

Taste with your tongue lickety lick
Reach with your finger flickety flick
Trickles down gutters
Gurgles down drains
Forming great big puddles
When it really rains

## Poems about wind

### Windy day

Why, oh why is the blue so high?
A windy day and clouds in the sky
I shall take out my kite and give it a try
Long tails streaming, just watch it fly.

### Windy words

*Try reading these words to children on a windy day. Talk about the sounds and sights the wind creates before they go out. Raise awareness before they go outside and then sit with them and listen to their ideas. Have a pen and paper ready to jot down what they say. A string of words can be a poem in itself or lead to something else. The exciting thing is that, like the wind, nobody knows where it will go.*

| | |
|---|---|
| Wind | roaring whooshing swooshing |
| Clouds | rushing hurrying scurrying |
| Leaves | dancing whirling twirling |
| Bins | banging clattering rattling |
| Trees | creaking swirling swaying |
| Wind | roaring whooshing swooshing |

### A windy walk on the beach

Wind in my fingers
Wind around my toes
It's blowing the sand
In my eyes, up my nose

Wind on my face
And wind around my ears
My eyes have caught the sand
It makes them full of tears

Wind in my hair
And wind on my back
We've turned around for home
And get blown along the track

## The breeze

Can you hear the gentle breeze
Rustling softly through the trees?
Dappled sunlight filters through
Dancing leaves of bright green hue

## Wind around my body

*Children need to hear the poem first and discuss any words that may be difficult. Four pictures showing trees, a street, a beach and a farm may be needed to help children who may have little or no English. After the first reading children can stand up and sway gently to and fro. At the last line of each verse they move or indicate the appropriate body part.*

Blow wind blow
Blow through the trees
Blow over the roof top
And blow around my knees

Blow wind blow
Blow along the street
Blow through the garden
And blow around my feet

Blow wind blow
Blow along the sands
Blow around the angry rocks
Blow around my hands

Blow wind blow
Blow through the farms
Blow around the grassy fields
Blow around my arms

## Wind on the beach

Sand is blowing, mind your eyes
Seaweed rolls across the sand
Waves white crashing rolling
Tumbling over with flecks of foam

## Wind in the country

It whistles round the roof tops, it whistles through the trees
It whooshes down the chimney stack and blows away the leaves
The grass is bending over and the branches swaying high
Look up and watch the fluffy clouds rushing through the sky.

## Wind in the town

*Children can learn this and add 'whoo' sounds at the beginning and end. It has a rhythmic beat and can be used with children of any age. Young children may like to stamp or clap.*

The wind is whistling down the street
Rubbish is whirling
Leaves are twirling
Swirling,
Curling
Round my feet

## Wind and waves

Where is the sea that we played in?
Where is the sea that lapped around our toes?
No gentle waves filling the sand castle moat
But a mighty thunder and waves turning
Rolling one after another
Pounding and swirling
White foam catching us where we stand
The surging endless rhythm of the waves

# The garden

## This is the way we plant our seeds

*This song can be sung to the tune of 'Here we go round the mulberry bush'. It can be used as it stands or children can add appropriate verses of their own according to the time of year.*

This is the way we plant our seeds, plant our seeds, plant our seeds,
This is the way we plant our seeds
As we work in our nursery garden

This is the we pick the flowers, pick the flowers, pick the flowers
This is the way we pick the flowers
As we work in the nursery garden.

This is the way we sweep up the leaves, sweep up the leaves, sweep up the leaves,
This is the way we sweep up the leaves
As we work in the nursery garden

This is the way we dig the ground, dig the ground, dig the ground
This is the way we dig the ground
As we work in the nursery garden

## What are we going to grow today?

*This poem may be sung to the tune of 'Here we go gathering nuts in May'. Children can do the actions as they sing.*

*Chorus*
What are we going to grow today?
Grow today, grow today
What are we going to grow today?
In our nursery garden.

We're going to plant some sunflowers high
Sunflowers high, sunflowers high
The tiny seeds will reach the sky
In our nursery garden

*Chorus*
We're going to water all our seeds
All our seeds, all our seeds
And gently pull out all the weeds
In our nursery garden

*Chorus*
We're going to dig potatoes out
Potatoes out, potatoes out
So get your spade and give a shout
In our nursery garden

*Chorus*
We're going to pick the strawberries red,
Strawberries red, strawberries red
And then we can eat them our teacher said
In the nursery garden

## Snowdrops

*A poem for older children. This could be read to a background of gently swaying music and children might want to move like the snowdrops in the breeze. Hopefully you will have some snowdrops growing somewhere in an outside space where they can find them for themselves. Always very exciting as the first snowdrops appearing herald the coming of spring.*

A pure white oval
Opens
Braving winter soil
Parading her green frilly petticoat
As she sways
Dancing in the winter wind

Dancing snowdrop
Long dark days
Pierced with snowdrop white
Sturdily
Mocking
Wind cold snow

## Daffodils

Daffodils nodding a spring time sight
Stars of yellow and stars of white
Trumpets orange and trumpets gold
They twist and turn through sun and cold

## Ten red tulips

*Use real or artificial flowers (change wording of the colour if necessary). Choose ten children from the group to hold a flower each and another ten to pick one. In a smaller group arrange flowers in a line in a container using floral foam. Use this with children who are working with numbers up to ten. They will enjoy adding some actions too.*

Ten red tulips standing in a line
Freddy came and picked one and that made nine
Nine red tulips near the garden gate
———— came and picked one and that made eight
Eight red tulips pointing up to heaven
———— came and picked one and that made seven
Seven red tulips standing near some sticks
———— came and picked one and that made six
Six red tulips glad to be alive
———— came and picked one and that made five
Five red tulips
———— came and picked one and that made four
Four red tulips nod towards a tree
———— came and picked one and that made three
Three red tulips wondering what to do
———— came and picked one and that made two
Two red tulips wide open in the sun
———— came and picked one and then were was one
One red tulip his life is nearly done
Gently dies back into the bulb and then there were none.

## Crocus

*Use this poem when you can have a bloom for children to look closely at, maybe with a magnifying glass. They will then learn and understand the meaning of the words 'petals' 'stamens' and 'anthers' as you discuss together what they see.*

A bed of crocus what a sight
Yellow purple gold and white
Stamens and anthers standing tall
Kept safe inside a petal wall
Bright and cheerful springtime flowers
Standing tall through sun and showers

## Growing carrots

The month of March is a good time to sow
Get out in the garden ready to grow
Open the packet and shake out some seeds
Fill pots with compost that has no weeds
Sprinkle the seeds with care on the top
Cover them gently to give a good crop
After two weeks some green leaves peep out
Water them carefully don't let them dry out
More leaves appear with feathery tops
Carrots are one of our favourite crops
As they grow bigger pull a few shoots
Small carrots are showing they're really the roots
Wash them carefully then take a bite
Cooked or raw they're a wonderful sight

## Growing potatoes

We laid out all the tubers
Carefully in a row
Light has helped the eyes
On our potatoes start to grow

But now it's time to dig a hole
And plant them in the ground
They need to go in very deep
The hole should be quite round

The soil is carefully put back in
Potatoes disappear
But they will grow and we can find
Lots more much later in the year

We'll water them and water them
Green leaves are growing tall
Small white flowers and then at last
Dig down deep to find them all

We use a spade to carefully dig
Moving the soil around
Searching for our harvest crops
Just guess what we have found

## Growing cucumbers

Crisp and crunchy, green and sweet
Home grown cucumbers are great to eat
In March the seeds were carefully sown
Tiny leaves, how they've grown
Each one was growing in its own pot
Watered each day they needed a lot
The plants have grown so very tall
They are half way up the garden wall
The yellow flowers came out in June
Plants are still growing and very soon
We will pick our cucumbers at the end of July
Cut them up so we can give them a try
Sandwiches big and sandwiches small
Cucumber sandwiches are best of all

## Planting beans

Put some bean seeds in a very large pot
Keep it warm but not too hot
After two weeks I can see some shoots
And under the soil there are long white roots
Water them gently every day
Plant then outside in the middle of May
A wigwam of sticks tied at the top
The beans climb up to give a good crop
Red flowers come out and petals fall
Insects pollinate the beans so small

Water them water them so they grow longer
Eating beans will help you get stronger
Some are curly and some are straight
But they taste so good they are worth the long wait

**My bean in a jar**

A clear pot or jar and a speckly brown bean,
Pink blotting paper – it must be clean,
I'll add some water and watch it each day
It needs light and warmth, so they all say.

A miracle happens – it's starting to grow,
The bean has split open and something just shows.
First to appear is a long white root
Then this is followed by a tiny green shoot.

The root hairs develop, I can see them well.
But my pink blotting paper is starting to smell.
The shoot's getting longer and longer each day
The leaves are unfolding and spreading both ways.

I measure its height with my ruler and tape,
My friend's bean is smaller, he's starting to gape
'What have you done? It's growing so high'
'I sing to it silly, so it won't die!'

It's taller than John's and the time has come
To plant it outside in the warm summer sun.
It's tied to a stick, and it's reaching so far
Who would have thought it – my bean in a jar

**Jasper's bean**

*This rap was composed with a group of children as a follow up to the story of Jasper's Beanstalk by Nick Butterworth.*

*It can be used after telling the story and after children have planted beans for themselves. Ask the children to stand up so they can sway and clap to the rhythm of the chorus which they will learn very quickly and be able to join in. Try composing a rap in similar style to follow another story.*

*Chorus*    Jasper, Jasper, the black and white cat
                He's not very thin in fact he's rather fat

On Monday morning he found a bean
He planted it deep nowhere to be seen

*Chorus*    Jasper, Jasper ————————
He dug it, he raked it, he sprayed it and he hoed it
He watered it well and then he even mowed it

*Chorus*    Jasper, Jasper ————————
He went out late on Friday night
Found the slugs and snails with his torch so bright

*Chorus*    Jasper, Jasper ————————
He got fed up because it wouldn't grow
Held it tight and gave a mighty throw

*Chorus*    Jasper, Jasper ————————
He went away and he read his book
Then out of the window he took one look

*Chorus*    Jasper, Jasper ————————
What did he see growing so tall?
His bean stalk had grown – after all!

*Chorus*    Jasper, Jasper, the black and white cat
He's not very thin, in fact he's rather fat

**My pot of weeds**

*Use this poem when you are planting cress. Read it before the children plant their seeds and then again just after planting and then again as the cress appears. By then the children will be used to the rhymes and the words and may join in with parts of the poem, in particular the spoken dialogue and the repeated last line.*

Crumbly brown earth goes into the pot
'Mind you don't spill it, you'll lose the lot'
Next we pick up the tiny new seeds
'I hope we don't grow a pot full of weeds!'

Teacher says we must scatter them low
But I know the posh word 'I'm going to sow'
Sewing on buttons? 'No I'm sowing seeds.
I hope we don't grow a pot full of weeds.'

I wait a few days, it's nearly a week
They're damp and warm, I must take a peek
Some tiny new shoots have appeared from my seeds.
'I hope I don't grow a pot full of weeds!'

I water them carefully and watch them grow
The leaves open out, but they're still very slow.
They suddenly spread, they look rather a mess.
'My pot hasn't grown weeds – it's full of green cress!'

## Planting lettuces

Today we're going to plant some seeds
Pots must be filled up to the top
With warm damp compost to help
To grow our lettuce crop

Today we're going to plant some seeds,
Take the packet and tear the top
Very carefully shake out a few
These will give us a lettuce crop

Today we're going to plant some seeds
Cover them up and water on top
Keep them warm and in a few days
We'll see small leaves of our lettuce crop

Today we're going to plant some seeds
After three weeks it's time to stop
The leaves will have grown
And then we can pick and eat our lettuce crop

## Strawberries

Tiny green plant with little green flowers
Place them in soil and wait for some showers
The petals drop off and the fruit starts to grow
Still small and hard they hang down in a row

Some days are cold and some days are hot
I do hope our plants are in the best spot
Sunshine and showers will make the fruit swell
And often we need to water as well

We check around for slugs and for snails
I do hope we won't find their silvery trails
A strawberry net will also be good
As birds love to peck at the fruit if they could

Pinky white first, then orange, then red
We must wait two more days our teacher just said
Then at last they are ready to eat
Our own home grown strawberries – what a fine treat

### Planting herbs

Lavender, thyme, mint and sage
Planting herbs is all the rage
We've added gravel to the ground
Dug the soil and mixed it round
Take the plant and firm it in
Water it well and growth will begin
Pinch off a leaf and take a smell
Fresh and pungent, our herbs will grow well.

## Senses in the garden

*The next five poems were written as a set. They can be read separately to fit in with something the children may have discovered or they can be used as a group over a period of several days if children are exploring the theme of the senses. Try to read each poem more than once and discuss with the children some of the sensory experiences that the poems evoke. Have a notepad handy and see if they can recall similar experiences. These can be recorded and may well lead to children creating their own poems.*

### The sense of smell

What did you **smell** in the garden today
As you ran outside eager to play?

I smelt the soil after the rain
Bonfire smoke tickled my nose
And I breathed in deep the smell of a rose

We're growing some herbs
They all have a smell
Lavender, rosemary, thyme as well

And I picked a sweet pea
A strong scented flower
The grass smelt damp after a shower

## The sense of touch

What did you **touch** in the garden today
As you ran outside ready to play?

My hands felt the bark of an old oak tree
Knobbly and rough, much taller than me
Soft wavy grasses tickled my nose
And I stroked the petals of a velvety rose

I turned over a log and touched a snail
A smooth shiny shell and a slimy trail
And then I found a smooth round stone
And under the pine tree a rough fir cone

## The sense of sound

What did you **hear** in the garden today?
As you ran outside eager to play?

My friends shouting, a laugh and a cry
An aeroplane engine high in the sky
But the most wonderful sound I ever heard
Was the deep throated song of a tiny bird.

The rustle of grasses waving in the breeze
And the wind as it rustles through all the leaves
Soft fall of rain on the roof and the ground
Leaves crunching frogs croaking – a wonderful sound.

## The sense of sight

What did you **see** in the garden today
As you ran outside eager to play?

Sunlight shimmering through the leaves
As they gently blow in the warm spring breeze
Shadows moving on the ground
And butterflies dancing all around

I saw my friends climbing up high
And an aeroplane trail across the sky
A tiny insect under a log
A millipede and a speckled green frog.

## The sense of taste

What did you **taste** in the garden today
As you ran outside ready to play?

I held out my tongue as the raindrops fell
They tasted so soft, and warm as well
Off to the raised beds to see what has grown
Pea pods are ready and lettuces sown

Apples are hanging down from the trees
Juicy and crunchy and so are the peas
But the best taste of all is the strawberry red
It waits to be picked from the strawberry bed.

## The tree

*This poem can be read after a discussion about the seasons. The starting point could be any remark by a child on the colour of leaves, the buds etc according to the season. There should be some discussion about the names of the seasons and looking at pictures of a tree through the year will support children who have English as an additional language*

At the bottom of my garden
Is a huge, enormous tree
And all through the year
He's a perfect friend for me

In spring the twigs point skywards
Swelling buds begin to show
And tips unfurl and open out
As leaves begin to grow

In summer time there's lot of leaves
A shady hiding place
I climb quite high to touch the sky
My own very special place

In autumn time the leaves change hue
From green to orange, yellow red
A windy day will blow them down
A scrunching crunching flowerbed

By winter time the leaves have gone
My tree is bare and stark
But from my bed, I see the moon
Shine through the branches dark.

# Garden creatures

### Butterfly finger rhyme

*If using with a baby make the butterfly shape with your hands and move them around above the baby's head. If using with a group of toddlers or older children they can make their own hands into the butterfly shape.*

Butterfly butterfly
Wings outspread
Butterfly flutterby
Over my head
Butterfly
Butterfly, butterfly what will you do?
Settle on flowers, yellow or blue
Dip your tongue in nectar sweet
Then flutter away in the summer's heat

### Ants

*Before reading this poem aloud to the children read it through to yourself to check out the voice parts. You will then be able to use different voice tones for the characters in the poem and as the children get to know the poem they will be able to do this too.*

'OH NO' says Mum,
I hear her shout.
'Come quickly Dad,
There's ants about'

She grabs for the spray
And starts to squirt,
'Do you have to do that Mum?
They really don't hurt.'

'They're crawling around
They'll get in the drawer,
They'll find all our food
And come back for more.'

'But Mum, they're only
Such tiny wee things,
And look over here,
Some have got wings.'

'Just get out of my way
While I give them a spray'
'Oh Mum please don't do that – PLEASE
I'll make them a home
Outside in the trees.

I'll catch them all now
And take them away
You won't see an ant
For many a day.

They'll be happier outside
They'll build a big nest.
Don't spray them please
Just give it a rest'

**Caterpillar moving**

Humping bumping
Caterpillar lumping
Up and over
The garden wall
Munching crunching
Caterpillar lunching
Juicy green leaves
Weeds and all

Wriggling, squiggling
Furling, curling
Round and round
In chrysalis ball

Itching twisting
Struggling pushing
Butterfly wings unfolding
Spreading out on the garden wall.

## The caterpillar

Creepy crawly caterpillar
Crawling up the tree
Creepy crawly caterpillar
Will you crawl to me?

Will you come and be my friend?
I'll keep you in a jar
Then you can come and live with me
And not crawl off too far.

I'll give you nuts and sweets to eat
You can grow quite fat
Now creepy crawly caterpillar
What do you think of that?

What's that you say?
You don't like sweets
You'd rather eat a nettle
And in my jar or in a box
You say you'll never settle

You say you're feeling funny
And very very fat
You're feeling very sleepy
What do you think of that?

You're looking very odd to me
You're really changing fast
Your little legs have disappeared
You're a chrysalis at last

Now creepy crawly caterpillar
I'll keep you safe from harm
And guard you through the winter time
Until it's really warm

And then you'll start to stretch a bit
While I watch with careful eye
You'll wriggle and twitch until
You become a butterfly

You'll float up on a gentle breeze
And flutter through the sky
Stretch your wings, such colourful things
A glorious butterfly.

## The centipede

What a good job
They don't wear shoes.
How many pairs
Would you need to choose?

Cent means a hundred
But I'm not sure
It really looks
As if he's got more.

He won't keep still
So we can count his feet
The centipede scuttles
Away down the street.

## The chrysalis

The chrysalis moves
It jerks, it twitches
It's jumping, it's turning
It's got the itches.

The colour is changing
It's cracking, it's splitting
A damp soggy bundle
Is pushing and hitting

Slowly it's stretching
Its beauty displaying
It's hanging and waiting
Resting and praying

It's drying and waiting
Growing much stronger
Wings are fluttering
How much longer?

At last it is flapping
Slowly, so slowly
Then suddenly lifting
And flying so gently.

At last it seems so far away
Fluttering up and up so high
Nothing remains but an empty skin
And a tiny speck in the deep blue sky.

**The robin**

Robin redbreast hopping around
Searching for crumbs lying on the ground

Robin redbreast perched on a spade
Spying worms in the hole I've made

Robin redbreast high in the tree
Chirrups his song especially for me

**Spider web (a poem for younger children)**

We were sitting in our garden
Just looking at the sky
When something rather special
Happened to catch my eye

Hanging from our tall green hedge
I saw a lovely sight
A spider's web was sparkling
With raindrops shiny bright

It's really very beautiful
My friends all came to see
Do you think we'll find the spider?
Wherever could he be?

Oh yes I think we've found him
He's curled up very tiny
He's waiting for some creature
To fly in his web so shiny

And then he will come dashing out
To see what he can see
And if it's something that he likes
He'll eat it for his tea

*These two poems are suitable for use with older children and can be used to stimulate discussion around the concept of the food chain as well as the beauty and shape of the spider web.*

## The web

Tiny dew droplets
Sparkling on
Fine misty spun threads
Too fine
Too beautiful
Yet still a menacing
Threat of death
To all unwary creatures

Death could not be
More precise
More beautiful
More inevitable

## The dilemma

Autumn mists
An early suspension
Of gossamer threads
A marvel of structure
Of style and symmetry
Mathematical precision
What a decision!

The spider's web is over my door.
I kneel down low and crawl on the floor!

## Squirrel

Over the fence and down on the ground
The squirrel scampers without a sound
He looks around for nuts or seeds
Nibbles some flowers and then some weeds
He goes to the feeder and searches the ground
Discovers a nut and glances around

Tufted ears twitch as he sits up to eat
His long bushy tail makes a soft comfy seat
Holds his nut in his tiny grey paws
Nibbles away then washes his claws
The meal is over, he runs up a tree
Sits on a branch and stares down at me

## A worm

Digging in the garden I came across a worm
I held him in my fingers
But he began to squirm
I gently put him down again
And watched him move along
He quickly wriggled down a hole
And very soon was GONE

## The earthworm

Eel like and wriggling
He slithers around,
Reeling and writhing,
With not even a sound
He buries his head
In the deep dark soil
Where he loves to hide
Away from us all.
Over the ground, he's not very slow
Rushing for cover before he's found
Making his tunnel under the ground.

**PLATE 2.01**   'Down to the beach down to the sea
Build a big sandcastle just for me'

'Down to the beach' – Summer

**PLATE 2.02**   'Then at last we can run down to the sea
Waves are sparkling as we jump in with glee'

'Going to the beach' – Summer

**PLATE 2.03**  'Here is a basket to gather them all'

'Conkers' – Autumn

**PLATE 2.04**  'What shall I do and where shall I go
I can't quite decide what to do in the snow'

'Out in the snow' – Winter

**PLATE 2.05**   'Tongue out
fresh smooth ice
tasting – nice'

'Senses in the snow' – Winter

**PLATE 2.06**   'A snowman just had to be made
A bright carroty nose
Stick arms and toes
And a body built with a spade'

'Snow' – Winter

**PLATE 2.07**  'Waterproof trousers, they're really good.
Getting them on is a bit of a struggle
but then I can search for a really large puddle'

'Playing in the rain' – Weather

**PLATE 2.08**  'Off to the woods and down the track
Push through the bracken – it's taller than me
Stop for a while under a tree'

'Forest school in autumn' – Life at nursery

**PLATE 2.09**  'A pure white oval
Opens
Braving winter soil
Parading her green frilly petticoat'

'Snowdrops' – The garden

**PLATE 2.10**  'We're going to dig potatoes out
So get your spade and give a shout'

'What are we going to grow today?' – The garden

**PLATE 2.11**    'Open the packet and shake out some seeds
Fill pots with compost that has no weeds'

'Growing carrots' – The garden

**PLATE 2.12**    'First to appear is a long white root
Then this is followed by a tiny green shoot'

'My bean in a jar' – The garden

**PLATE 2.13** 'Humping bumping
Caterpillar lumping'

'Caterpillar moving' – Garden creatures

**PLATE 2.14** 'Will you come and be my friend?'

'The caterpillar' – Garden creatures

**PLATE 2.15**  'Red paint, blue paint, yellow paint and green
The brightest colours you've ever seen
The paper is full but I haven't quite done
So I'll paint my hands – one by one'

'Painting' – Life at nursery

**PLATE 2.16**
'Would you like to see my den?
It's got a roof and windows too'
'Would you like to see my den?' –
Life at nursery

## The ladybird

Six black spots
A back of red
Six little legs
And a shiny black head

Just a ladybird
You may say
But keep on looking
For many a day
And you will find
Ladybirds of a different kind

Some have ten spots
Some have two
Some are yellow
But none are blue.

Some are black
With yellow spots
Make a record
And you'll find lots

A hundred species
Are recorded
Just find ten
You'll be rewarded!

## The nest

We've put a nest box in our garden
Fixed up high on an old oak tree
Some nuts hang down on a nearby branch
To tempt the birds to come and see

And then one day one flew inside
Out popped his head he looked around
Then off he flew but came back soon
Beakful of grass and moss he'd found

We watch the nest box every day
The blue tits flying to and fro
They carry insects in their beaks
So baby birds can feed and grow

And when the baby birds have flown
We carefully peep inside the box
A nest so tiny and so neat
Made of twigs and hair and moss

## The slug

Slimy slippery
Slowly crawling
Slug
Crispy, crunchy
Scrunchy, munchy
Lettuce
Who will win
The slug
Or me?
Wait and see

## The snail

'I don't want to wake up' said the snail
As he hid in his curly brown shell
'It's too hot today and I don't feel well
And I've got to carry this heavy old shell!'

'I'm not very happy I'll go back to bed
I'll seal up my shell and hide my head'

But the sun goes in and the raindrops fall
The garden's all damp and he wants to crawl
The grass is moist and it's getting wetter,
Our friend the snail is feeling much better

He pokes out his head
And his eyes on a stalk
His slimy brown tail uncurls as well
For he cannot walk

He slides and he glides as he carries his shell
Straight off to the lettuces, curly and sweet
For a tasty fresh meal of leaves, juicy and sweet.

**Under the log**

Slowly I lift the heavy damp log
Something jumps out, a tiny wee frog,
I lay the log down on the nearby ground
I must move carefully and not make a sound.

Now what can I see wriggling around,
Tiny earthworms, fat, pink and round.
There are grey creeping woodlice and creatures small,
Shiny black beetles, minibeasts all.

'Oh look miss, he's got so many feet'
'It's a millipede children, isn't he sweet'
And look in the corner, a little brown snail
Curled up in his shell, he's really quite frail.

They're all rushing around frightened and dazed
There's really so many, I'm quite amazed.
It's time to go in and put back the log
So carefully and gently, but where is the frog?

We hunt high and low, and search all around,
Then suddenly spot him, I'm so glad he's found.
I hope when we've gone, he'll hop back to his home
He needs to find shelter until he's full grown.

# Life at nursery

**Starting nursery school**

I'm going to school,
I'm not at all sure
There's so many people
When I go through that door.

I'm feeling so nervous
And a little bit shy.
I don't want to go,
But I don't know why.

Mummy is talking,
'Now stop being silly,
Look here are some toys,
And there's Joanna and Billy'

'But I don't want to play
I just want my mummy
I really could do with
My teddy and dummy'

The teachers are smiling
There's lots of nice toys.
The teachers are kind to
The girls and the boys

My mummy sits down
She's playing with trains
There's cars and there's dolls
And all sorts of games

Now I look round
It's not really so bad
I'm going to paint
A bright picture for Dad

My teacher is reading
From a nice new book
She says we will sing
And learn to cook.

There's so much to do
I think I might stay
But it's time to go home
And come back the next day.

**School**

I'm going to school,
I don't want to be late,
I let go of my mummy
And run to the gate

Here's my own peg,
I take off my hat
Hang it up carefully
Wipe my feet on the mat.

I'll go straight inside
And get on with my play
'Bye, bye Mummy
See you later today!'

**Choices**

What shall I play with at school today?
There's paint on the table and sand in the tray
On the floor I can see a train
And I really love playing outside in the rain

Or maybe I'll quietly look at a book
Draw a picture or even cook
I must remember to have my snack
There's a special table there at the back

What have I done at school today?
Water and sand are my favourite play
And when it's time to pack up the toys
My teacher will ask us girls and boys
What have you played with at school today?

**Nursery days by Anne Addo**

You ask the question all the time,
'What did you do today?'
But mum you ought to know by now
I come here just to play!

I've made castles in the sandpit,
And made the biggest one,
Once I'd finished building that,
It felt like time to run.

I chased my friends for ages,
Acting like a dinosaur,
And every time I got quite close,
I gave a mighty ROAR!

After that we had a break;
Some fruit, then milk to drink
Sitting there with my best friend,
It gave me time to think.

A quick play with the instruments,
We played, just like a band
Then I took myself to toilet
And yes ...I washed my hands!

Then my teacher called me;
My turn to write my name.
I tried my best and after that
She let me play a game.

I painted a nice picture
With red and green and blue
I'm giving it to grandma...
She loves everything I do!

## Please can I be your friend?

I want to be your friend
I know I'm a girl and you're a boy
But I'd really like to share your toy
Please can I be your friend?

I want to be your friend
My parents come from a far off land
I do not always understand
The words you say, the games you play,
Please can I be your friend?

I want to be your friend
My legs are weak and yours are strong
My chair needs help to push it along
Please will you be my friend?

## Painting

Red paint, blue paint, yellow paint and green
The brightest colours you've ever seen
A swirl of red and a dash of blue
I'm doing a painting just for you
Painting is really so much fun
The paper is full but I haven't quite done
So I'll paint my hands – one by one

## Let's pretend

I'm going to nursery school to play
I'm not sure what I'll be today.

I could be a cowboy
Or a pirate bold
Sail in my ship
To search for gold

I might be a doctor
And make you better
Or a postman who brings you
A lovely letter

I might be a fireman
With ladder and hose
Or a jolly clown with
A bright red nose

But whatever I choose I know you will say
'What did you do at school today?'

**A trip to the moon**

I'm taking my dog to the moon today
It's cold in space and I'll need my suit
Shall I take sausages
And maybe some fruit?

I might need a phone
And maybe a book
Fuel for the rocket
A saucepan to cook

Who's coming with me?
Timmy and Sue
My dog is barking
Blast off is due.

Count down is starting
54321
The engines are firing
The journey's begun

Soon we are zooming
Up into the air
Over our playground
The wind's in my hair

Now we are landing
It's time for our lunch
Sausages first and
An apple to crunch.

We'll chat to the men
Who live on the moon
They love having friends
So we'll return again soon.

## Just for me

What shall I do at school today?
When I arrive and go off to play
My favourite things
Are the blocks made of wood
And nobody tells me what I should
Do or what I should say
They just let me play.

Then it's up to me to decide
Whether to make a horse to ride
A car to drive or a plane to fly
And nobody comes to ask me why.

## Going out on a bus

*This poem was written by a group of children as we sat on an imaginary bus. We sang it to a tune that vaguely resembled 'Lord of the dance'*

We're all going to the fair
What do you think we could do there?
We'll ride on roundabouts and swing on swings
And do lots of other exciting things

We're all going to the shops
We'll buy some sweets and lollipops
When we're tired an ice cream too
We might even buy an extra one for you

We're all going to the park
We might stay there until its dark
We'll play some games and feed the ducks
Before we go home on the big red bus

## Down the winding path in the garden

Nobody knows
Where I go to play
As I quietly walk
And secretly talk
Down the winding path in the garden

Nobody knows
There's a castle of twigs
And an army of kings
Oh so many things
Down the winding path in the garden

Nobody knows
Where I talk to the trees
Sing to the breeze
And pick up leaves
Down the winding path in the garden

Nobody knows
I've my own little house
With a cupboard and bed
And the clouds overhead
Down the winding path in the garden

## My friend

Why don't you stay inside today?
It's very cold and looks like rain
The room is warm and you could choose
To look at a book or play with a train

Oh no I really have to go outside
I need to find my special den
Twigs and stones and a leafy roof
I built it yesterday just before ten

And later that day I made a friend
He said he'd be back there today
So if you don't mind I really must go
My dinosaur is coming to play

### Would you like to see my den?

Would you like to see my den?
It's got a roof and windows too
A door at the front and one at the back
But I forgot to make a place for a loo

We've got a kitchen and a little shelf
Twigs and sticks to use as forks
We need to collect some cones and moss
When we go to the woods on one of our walks

### Forest school in autumn

Wellies raincoats and gloves are cool
We wear them for our forest school
Off to the woods and down the track
Over the brambles with fruits so black
Push through the bracken – it's taller than me
Stop for a while under a tree
Take a breath and look around
Listen carefully to the forest sound
Leaves are stirring fanned by the breeze
Floating down gently from the tall oak trees
Not much is moving as we stand so still
And then we hear the robins trill
The leaves are wet as we scrunch along
Still listening to the robin's song.

### Making birdcake

*Use the name of a nursery practitioner in verse 2.*

Quick, quick we're going to make
A very special sort of cake
We need some seeds, some grated cheese
Bread and apple, oh yes please!

And now Miss ——— has got some fat,
The heat is on and fancy that,
It's going all runny, it's melting quick.
So stir it in the mixture thick.

We'll stir it round and round and round
We're all so busy, there's not a sound
And now it's stirred it goes in the pot
Be very careful – it's still quite hot.

Now it goes in the fridge to cool
Yes we've got a fridge in our nursery school
And when it's set really hard,
All the bits and the melted lard
We go outside and stretch to the sky
Hang the birdcake nice and high

We creep inside and watch so still
The birds fly down to eat their fill
A blue tit, a great tit, a robin red,
When it's so cold, they love to be fed.

# Celebrations and festivals

## Poems for Christmas

### Baubles and stars

Christmas tree Christmas tree
Time to decorate the Christmas tree
Baubles silver, red and gold
Smooth and shiny, gently hold
One for you and one for me
And then at last
On the top of the tree
A shiny star for all to see

### The Christmas tree

Here comes the tree – make sure it stands straight
Wrap round the lights then decorate
Little gold stars, bells that tinkle
Baubles that shine and baubles that twinkle
Now we have finished, stand back and see
What a wonderful sight this Christmas tree
Switch on the lights and watch them shine
Through the branches so strong and fine
Starbright candles twinkle and shine
Which of those presents do you think is mine?

They lie waiting under the tree
Some are for you and some are for me.
Some are for nana and grandpa too
With labels and ribbons, silver and blue
Some are quite big and others quite small
Some are short and others are tall
Parcels of every shape and size
It's a wonderful sight for my gazing eyes

**Nativity play**

Please come and watch our nativity play
It's about a star that lost its way
Her friends went travelling one very dark night
And disappeared right out of sight
She stopped at Bethlehem and twinkled so bright
She filled the sky with a heavenly light

Please come and watch our nativity play
The stage fills with angels singing away
They all look so sweet with halos and wings
And they talked to the shepherds of stables and kings
They all wear white dresses and one of them sings
About stars and babies and those sorts of things

Please come and watch our nativity play
Shepherds watch sheep through night and through day
The angels appear to them on top of the hill
'Please go to Bethlehem if you will'
So they follow the angels a very long way
To the stable in Bethlehem far far away

Please come and watch our nativity play
Three kings who arrive from lands far away
They all wear their crowns
And presents they bring
Gold frankincense myrrh
Fit for a king

Please come and watch our nativity play
There's a sheep that goes baa and donkeys that bray
The animals gather around the manger
Keeping the baby safe from danger
Visitors come to see this new little stranger

As Mary and Joseph watch over the manger

Please come to watch our nativity play
And see baby Jesus asleep on the hay

## Poems about Chinese New Year

### Chinese New Year

*This poem can be said or sung to the tune of Frere Jacques.*

Fiery dragons
Fiery dragons
Red and gold
Red and gold
Twitching writhing turning
Twitching writhing turning
Chinese New Year

### New Year

*Fill in the first line with the appropriate animal.*

It's the year of the ————
The New Year is here
And we need to celebrate
This new Chinese Year

Mandarin oranges
A special treat
As firecrackers
Explode around our feet

Special music, a special dance
As the fiery dragon comes to prance
Head held high and shiny scales
Writhing body and a spiky tail

Gifts are given wrapped in shiny red
Sometimes money or sweets instead
We wear our best clothes to visit our friends
As one year begins and the other one ends

## Poems about bonfire night

### Five little fireworks

*This is a simple version using the same three lines for each verse and can be used with younger children.*

Five little fireworks standing in a row
Please be very careful how you go
A grown up lights one and it shoots up high
Bursts into stars and lights the night sky

Four little fireworks standing in a row
Please be very careful how you go
A grown up ————————
Three little etc etc
Two little etc
One little etc

*This version is more complex and suitable for slightly older children as there are more words to learn.*

Five little fireworks lying on the floor
A grown up comes to light one and that makes four

Four little fireworks are grouped beside a tree
A grown up lights a sparkler and that makes three

Three little fireworks not sure what to do
A grown up lights the Catherine wheel and that leaves two

Two little fireworks are waiting for some fun
A grown up lights the candle star and that leaves one

One little firework wants to go so far
A grown up lights the rocket and he shoots up to the stars

### Bonfire night

Spinning circles
Dazzle
Bright against the dark night
Roman candle
Fountains of gold

Shimmer and sparkle
Falling like rain
Stars exploding
Slowly fading
Leaving the moon

**Bonfire and fireworks**

*This poem was written by a small group of children. The adults noted down what had impressed the children most on bonfire night and they discussed together the order of the poem choosing the lines as they appear below. You could try asking a group of children to recall their experiences in a similar way and then read this poem to them either before or after transcribing their ideas.*

Smoke curls twist upwards
Showers of sparks
Gold against the blue black sky
Catherine wheels spin
Rockets explode
Flashing star balloons
Red and white and blue and gold

**Fifth of November**

*Read this with lots of expression. Use an excited tone at the beginning and read fairly quickly but slowing down as you go on and then say the last line very slowly with heavy rhythm.*

It's bonfire night
Children excited
Squeal with delight
Put on your gloves
Where is your hat?
A scarf round your throat
And a warm winter coat

Screaming rockets
Exploding so bright
Coloured stars shining
Amidst the dark night

Catherine wheels spin
An explosion of light
Fiery gold circles
A wonderful sight

Sparklers twinkle
As we wave them around
I like them best
They don't make a sound

Fountains explode
Green red and white
Shimmering rain
Smoke filled night

## The bonfire

Blazing bonfire
Crackling twigs
Golden sparks
Shoot high
Dark velvet sky

## Firework safety

Fireworks can be a little bit scary
And even the grownups should be extra wary
Put gloves on your hand as a sparkler you hold
Against the night sky it shoots stars of gold.
Swirling and whirling they're really good fun
They crackle and sparkle then they are done
But always remember they're still very hot
Put them down gently in a special spot.
Light the blue touch paper stand well clear
Watch grownups do this and don't stand too near
The fireworks will glow and then suddenly whoosh
Afar up in the sky right over our bush
The stars just go on through the night sky
Exploding and shimmering way up high
And then it's all over the fire's getting low
Fireworks are finished it's time to go

### My rocket

My rocket is ready
It stands in the ground
Dad lights the blue touch paper
Wait for the sound
A sudden loud whoosh
A gold trail a mass of gold stars
A sudden loud bang
Will it reach Mars?

### Bonfire sparklers

*This poem should be used with older children and will make a useful starting point for discussion about firework safety. Children should only hold a sparkler with an adult and even then must be very careful. Children can act this out in the classroom holding imaginary sparklers.*

November is here, it's the time of the year
Bonfires, toffee and sparklers to hold
Write your name in sparkling gold
Twist it turn it taking care
Hold your sparkler in the air
Keep it away and hold it tight
Make some circles a dazzling sight

## A birthday poem

### My birthday

How many sleeps til my birthday?
You say it's only three
I'm getting really excited
I can hardly eat my tea

How many sleeps til my birthday?
Now its only two
I'm getting so excited
I don't know what to do!

How many sleeps til my birthday?
At last it's only one
When I wake up in the morning
The day will be filled with fun

Now today is my birthday!
My friends are coming to tea
There's presents on the table
Are they really all for me?

And now it's time for my party
My friends begin to arrive
Light the candles on the cake
One, two, three, four, five!

# Pets

## My dog

I love to take him to the park
We play together until its dark
I love to take him to the beach
And throw a ball beyond his reach
I love to take him on the sand
We chase and play – it's really grand
I love to take him to the sea
He splashes and swims together with me
I love to take him down the street
He's well behaved and walks at my feet
But best of all is when I take him to bed
And he curls round my feet and I can stroke his head.

## Puppy

Black snuffly nose
Black eyes
Velvet ears
Paws that seem too big
And the waggiest tail in the world

### A dog

*This poem has been written in the style of a kenning. (See page 5 in Chapter 1, What is poetry?) Older children might be able to have a go at something like this but may need help to reverse the word order to start with. They will need to hear kennings written by other poets and discuss the essential poetic structure of using the noun before the adjective.*

Tail wagging
Nose snuffling
Paws scratching
Eyes begging
Here comes my ——————- dog

### My cat

My cat stretches
Paws unfold
Claws unfold
Her body long
Upon the chair

### My cat curls

My cat curls
Head into a ball
Tail into a ball
Only a whisker shows
Upon the chair

### Kitten

*This poem was written together with the help of a group of five-year-olds.*

How can you be
So sweet?
Fluffy ball
Chasing leaves
Sleeping
Purring
Spiky tail
Whiskers neat

### My cat stretches

*This poem can be used with younger children. As they listen to the words they may wish to act out the movements of the cat. Older children can listen to the structure of the poem. They may be encouraged to write a poem like this. There is no need for rhyme but the repeated last line in each verse lends structure. It should be read slowly as if to emphasis the deliberate movements of the cat.*

My cat stretches
Paws unfold
Claws uncurl
Tail hangs low
Her body long
Upon the chair

My cat curls
Head into ball
Tail around ball
Only a whisker
Reaching out
Upon the chair

### The cat

Silky smooth
His fur is soft
Warm like silk
Ears of velvet
His whiskers are long
And they twitch as he
Laps up his milk
His tail curls round him
When he sleeps by the fire
But when he is happy
He holds it up higher

### The hunting cat

Silently stalking
Prowling not walking
He's not really a pet
More of a hunter
Lying so still
Then silently springing
Pouncing and jumping

Suddenly darting
He's not really mine
When he tries to kill

But suddenly turning
He strolls over to me
My heart is yearning
His heart is purring
Tail high in the air
He rubs against me
Come on in cat
It's time for your tea.

## My goldfish

I know he's only a goldfish
But I love him just the same
He swims to the top of the water
Whenever I whisper his name.

His tail is black
But his fins are gold
I've had him for ages
So he must be quite old

His scales are shiny
And neatly arranged
And every week
The water is changed

I move all the stones
And replant the weed
Then he swims to the top
For his daily feed

I know he's only a goldfish
But I love him just the same

## My fish tank

I keep my fish in a very large tank,
It stands on a shelf in our room
It has its own light which I can switch on
So the fish shine out from the gloom

Some of the tetras are little blue fish
Which even glow in the dark
We've got guppies and mollies and angel fish too
But my favourite is Ruby – the little red shark!

## My new pet

*For the last line teacher and children could choose a name preferably the name of a
hamster they know.*

Whatever is in that little blue box?
Is it a kitten or a baby brown fox?
It's moving and scurrying round and round
I really don't know what you have found.

May I peep in? I'll keep very quiet.
It's a hamster! Oh Mum where did you buy it?
It's got such red eyes and tiny sharp feet
Oh Mum, he's a beauty and really sweet.

Now where can he live? We must buy him a cage.
He's still quite a baby – what is his age?
He's soft and he's silky, cuddly and warm
I promise I'll keep him safe from harm

Oh Mum you're so wonderful – he's really the best
I'll look after him carefully, he won't be a pest.
I'll feed him, and clean him and help him to play
And when I'm at school he will sleep through the day.

I'll give him a name now. What shall we choose?
Hammy or Frederick or a name from the news.
He's not very good, he's really quite bad
………………..'s the best name for such a bad lad.

## My rabbit

She lives all day in her wooden hutch
But gladly runs to me
She snuffles out her pleasure
When I offer her her tea

Her nose is wibbly wobbly
And her whiskers are so long

She loves to eat her carrots
They make her grow so strong

I love to stroke her velvet coat
And gently pull her ears
She really understands my smiles
And wipes away my tears

Her golden coat is silky,
Her ears, they feel the same
She's a very special rabbit
And AMBER is her name.

## My pony

Gently I stroke his knotted mane
Tangled by wind and dampened by rain
His eyes are restless but he stands so still
Dare I mount him – Yes I will

'Whoa there Rob' I don't mean to harm
We'll go down the track and past the farm
Then up on the hill on the stony lane
When we get home I can brush your mane

Now that's much better I'm enjoying the ride
The hills stretch before us open and wide
You're plodding along 'Shall we try a trot?'
Gently, now gently past this spot

Now slowing down near the rock like a table
We're nearly home and back in the stable
A bucket of mash, some nice warm hay
I promise I'll be back another day.

## Wild pony

*A poem suitable for older children particularly those who may have seen wild ponies on our hills, moors and forests. It may lead on to some further discussion and maybe some creative work.*

Wild as wind he gallops free,
Over the hill past the dark tree
Tail and mane streaming

Bright eyes gleaming
Why oh why won't he wait for me?

His life is the mountains,
The heather topped hill
The shelter of rock
When the wind blows chill.

The warmth of the sun
On his speckled back
The damp of the mist
As he finds the track

It leads him home
His home on the hill
Why won't he wait?
Perhaps one day he will.

# Colours

## Multicolours

### Balloons

*This is a good poem to use with younger children. If you are able to use some coloured balloons it will keep their attention as they hear the rhyming verses.*

My new balloon is such a bright red
I'll tie it up on the end of my bed

My new balloon is a brilliant blue
I can hold it tight and then throw it to you

My new balloon is a shiny fresh green
The most beautiful shade you've ever seen

My new balloon is a yellow so bright
It looks just like the sun – a glorious sight!

My new balloon is a purple so deep
I dream I am holding it when I'm asleep

My new balloon is a gleaming white
It's got a long string for me to hold tight

My new balloon is a shocking pink
This is MY favourite – what do you think?

### Colours in the fridge

I open the fridge
What a surprise
A paint box of colours
Greets my eyes

Lettuces green
And eggs of brown
I didn't know Mummy
Had been to town

A bag of tomatoes,
So red and shiny
Some frozen green peas
They're really quite tiny

There's three pints of milk
Creamy and white
And a box of six yoghurts
With colours so bright

There's a big pack of butter
It's a beautiful yellow
And a punnet of peaches
With flesh ripe and mellow

What's that at the back?
Juicy grapes in a bunch
A lovely dark purple
Delicious for lunch

There's two kinds of apples
Some green and some red
Round oranges bright
I can't wait for bed

For then I can choose
For my bedtime treat
Something so special
From the fridge to eat

**The multicoloured granny**

A scarf of purple
A coat of red
A hat of yellow
Is on her head

Her skirt is blue
And her shoes are green
She's the brightest old lady
I've ever seen.

Her stockings are brown
Her gloves are pink
Her blouse is………..
Well what do you think?
Of course you are right
It has to be …..WHITE!

**Coloured slippers**

My new slippers are a very bright green
I keep them safe where they cannot be seen

My new slippers are a very bright red
I keep them safe under my bed

My new slippers are a shiny black
I keep them safe out at the back

My new slippers are a very deep blue
They live in the bathroom
But not near the loo

### Coloured wellies

I've got some wellies
They're shiny and red
I take them off
When I go to bed

I've got some wellies
They're shiny and blue
I don't want to wear them
They're so brand new

I've got some wellies
They're such a bright pink
They go in the cupboard
Under the sink

I've got some wellies
They're sort of dark green
I stamped in the mud
Now they're not very clean

I've got some wellies
Mine are deep black
Too small to begin with
They had to go back

Now I've got bigger ones
They fit me just right
Just look at our wellies
What a bright cheerful sight.

## Black

Black is dark
Black is coal
A deep glossy shine
Of a newborn foal
Black is a mood
Of sadness and gloom
Black are the corners
Of a smoke filled room

Black is a cat
A stroke of good luck
Blackness of feathers
On a tufted duck
Black is the ink
On a page of white
But blackest of black
Is a moonless night!

**********************************

**Black** is the colour of lumps of coal
The jet black coat of a newborn foal
Black is the colour of birds that sing
Swallows and swifts as they dart on the wing
Black is the colour of a Friesian cow
Stripy zebra, and an old black sow.
Black is the colour of ebony beads
And black is the colour of onion seeds
Black is the colour of a moonless night
The creepy black that fills you with fright
Black is the tip of a frost bitten leaf
Black is the colour of sadness and grief

**Black and white**

Two black eyes on a face of white
The giant panda's a favourite sight
But look over there on the frozen ground
Black and white penguins waddle around
And hiding so carefully behind the trees
The stripy zebras that everyone sees

Then out of the zoo, and onto the street
A black and white crossing, step on with your feet
A black and white pole, a black and white cat
A wagtail, a magpie, a black and white hat
Black lamb in the field of sheep so white
Snow on dark trees on a winter's night
Black ink stares up from a snow white sheet
And a liquorice allsort is really a treat.

## Blue

Sapphires sparkling on a necklace fair
Blue forget me knots tied in my hair
But none can give me such a surprise
As the piercing blue of Grandad's eyes

*********************************

*As you read this next poem wait for the children to join in at the end. It would be helpful to have had some discussion about the shades of blue using different objects and photographs. Children can use paint and coloured pens in different shades of blue to create their pictures.*

Azure, topaz, sapphire
Navy, turquoise and aquamarine,
They're names of a colour – it isn't green
Royal and powder, can you guess
They are shades of ————— YES YES YES

*********************************

A tiny baby is dressed in blue
Rompers and bootees all brand new
He soon grows older and wears blue shorts
Then blue school clothes and outfits for sports
Then into his teenage uniform
Blue denim of course is all that is worn

*********************************

Sparkling, shining, shimmering sea
The blue waves dance in front of me
I lie on the sand and look up on high
White seagulls soaring against a blue sky

## Brown

Brown is the colours of the things of the ground
Rabbits and creatures that make no sound
Out of their dens in the dark brown earth
When springtime calls to give them new birth
New lives, new adventures to be found

\*\*\*\*\*\*\*\*\*\*\*\*\*\*\*\*\*\*\*\*\*\*\*\*\*\*\*\*\*\*\*\*\*\*

Velvety chocolates in an expensive box
The orange brown coat of a fleeting fox
Gnarled old tree trunks grow out of brown soil
Shiny brown conkers for the autumn spoil

**Green**

Grass is growing so fresh and green
Rivers are flowing as fast as I've seen
Emeralds are glowing fit for a Queen
Spring breezes blowing, fresh and clean
Now it's springtime and winter has been

**Green in springtime**

Green speckled skin
On a golden eyed frog
Emerald green moss
On a dark damp log

Green buds uncurling
Green shoots unfurling
New leaves are growing
And the grass needs mowing!

# Grey

Grey is the colour of uniform shirts
Of little boy's trousers and girls long grey skirts

Grey is the colour of an elephant's skin
From his long floppy ears to his tail so thin

Grey is the colour of our school's pet mouse
And grey is the colour on the wall of our house

\*\*\*\*\*\*\*\*\*\*\*\*\*\*\*\*\*\*\*\*\*\*\*\*\*\*\*\*\*\*\*\*\*\*

Grey skies hang heavy
Over my head
The clouds are gathering
It looks like lead

The slate roofs and pavements
Of the grey town
Are shining with rain
As it pours down

## Orange

Orange is the setting sun
A glowing sky when day is done
Reflecting over wavy sea
An orange path leads back to me

*********************************

Orange fruit on the grocer's stall
Pomegranates peaches and mellow plums
Satsumas and mandarins when winter comes
But a juicy orange is best of all

*********************************

Orange is my favourite
It's the only colour you can really eat
It's round and juicy
What a treat
It's not a fish and it's not a meat
It's the name of a fruit that's not always sweet

*********************************

Orange leaves on autumn trees
Come swirling and curling down
They lie on the ground
An orange sea
Walk through it
What a sound
Crunching and crackling
Rustling and shuffling
Scrunching and scuffling

**Orange is**

The colour of leaping flames in the fireplace
Of sunset streaks in a dark blue sky
Fresh carrots pulled from brown earth
A dustcart as it ambles by.

*After the children have heard this poem it might be possible for them to think of another poem and write a poem in a similar style. Again, it does not have to rhyme. It is more important that they are using their imagination and choosing some good descriptive words.*

**********************************

Oranges, clementines, satsumas, mandarins
So many names but all one colour
Deep glowing richness of orange fruit

Acer, chestnut, sycamore, beech, oak
Leaves of gold and bronze
The bright flaming colours of an orange autumn

## Pink

Pink is a rosebud
A baby's nails
White mice with pink eyes
And long pink tails

**********************************

Ice cream is pink
And lollipops too
I like candy floss
How about you?

**********************************

Pink is the colour for baby girls
Pink bonnets pink bootees and ribbons for curls
Pink bunches of flowers, pink fingers and toes
Pink rosy cheeks and a snub pink nose

## Purple

Plums are ripening high up in a tree
As soon as they're purple, please pick one for me.
Purple violets are shy little flowers,
They peep through the grass as they wait for the showers

Deep velvet pansies are strong bright and gay
They nod their faces all through the day
Bunches of grapes on the market stall
Are the purple fruit I like best of all

*********************************

Purple is the colour of kings
Of shy little violets and butterflies wings

Mauve or violet indigo blue
Are all different shades of a purple hue

Deep velvet pansies and shiny plums
Purple paint on my finger and all over my thumbs.

## Red

Red is the colour of danger
Stop, look and listen and don't rush on
Red is the colour of danger

Red is the colour of ripeness
Apples, tomatoes, red peppers and plums
Red is the colour of ripeness.

Red is the colour of sunset
Of storms and sky at night
Red is the colour of sunset

Red is the colour of warmth
The leaping flames of a cosy fire
Red is the colour of warmth

Red is the colour I like best of all
My lunch box, my curtains and bedroom wall
Red is the colour I like best of all

**Red in nature**

Robin sings from the top of the tree
Red breast fluffed out for all to see.
Red admiral rests on a scented flower
Sipping nectar hour by hour
Poppies scarlet between the corn
A fiery red sky before a storm

## Yellow

Yellow sand for miles and miles
Yellow teeth as an old woman smiles
Yellow buttercups reflecting the sun
A yellow sky when day is done

*********************************

Yellow is bright and cheerful and gay
It can be seen clearly on a dark wet day
Yellow is the colour of safety hats
A fireman's helmet and my brand new mac

*********************************

A gleam of yellow in the spring
A primrose peeping or a bluetit's wing
Sweet fluffy chickens scratching the ground
Long dangling catkins dancing around

*********************************

Yellow buttercups under my chin
Reflecting their colour onto my skin
Yellow as butter – yellow they shine
But they are outshone by the celandine

# Rhymes and rhythms

*The poems in this section can all be used to illustrate a particular aspect of poetic form as well as just being enjoyed for the sounds of the words and the rhythmic feel. A poem with a strong rap rhythm 'Jasper's bean' is included in The garden section.*

### Animal alphabet alliteration

Alfie is an alligator
Bertie is a bear
Colin is a caterpillar
With very fuzzy hair

Danny is a spotty dog
Eric is an elephant
Freddie is a freckly frog
Gary is a greedy goat
Herbert is a hairy hog

Ivan is an iguana
Who gobbles lots of flies
Joshua's a jaguar
Beware his golden eyes

Katie is a kangaroo
She jumps around the place
Lenny is a roaring lion
His mane hangs round his face

Michael is a monkey
Swinging from the trees
Nancy is a nanny goat
With very knobbly knees

Ollie is an octopus
Eight tentacles curl round
Percy is a porcupine
With spines that touch the ground

Queenie is a quail
That is a bird quite rare
Robert is a rhino
With horn and eyes that stare

Susie is a spotty seal
She lives deep in the sea
Terry is a tortoise
Who lives at home with me

Ursula eats ugli fruit
Violet likes vanilla
William is a large white whale
And can be a fearsome killer

X is just a letter sound
That's very hard to rhyme
Yasmin is a yellow yak
Long coat and horns so fine

Zak could be a zebra
Living in the zoo
And that concludes the alphabet
With love from me to you.

### Dinosaur

*This should be read first to the children. Enjoy the sound of the words as you read and then talk about the way the words just follow on from each other with no verbs. Read it again and then ask them to give ideas of words. Maybe start off a new poem that they can join in, perhaps with another type of dinosaur e.g. brontosaurus, stomping clomping etc.*

Triceratops
Lumbering
Clumbering
Clambering

Tail lashing
Thrashing
Small eye
Flashing

Neck
Stretching
Swaying
Youngster playing

Nostrils
Twitching
Skin
Itching

Spikes
Heaving
Head
Turning

Eyes
Burning

## A counting rhyme about dinosaurs

Five fierce dinosaurs stomped along the shore
Along came a carnivore and that left four

Four fierce dinosaurs swimming in the sea
One met a brachiosaur and that left three

Three fierce dinosaurs playing peek a boo
One took fright and ran away and that left two

Two fierce dinosaurs were having lots of fun
One lay down and went to sleep and that left one

One fierce dinosaur exploring on his own
Fell into a mammoth trap and that left none.

## Names, phonics and rhymes

*These are a few examples to get you started on working with children. They could listen to a few of these and then begin to work with you using their own names. Lots of encouragement for trying!*

Joshua Jones likes jelly and jam
Herbert Hill likes hamburgers and ham

Billy travels in buses and boats
Gary likes grasshoppers, geese and goats

Alice likes apples, alligators and ants
Pauline wears pink, even her pants

Molly eats melon, mandarins and mango
Tim's favourite dance is a very fast tango

Carol craves cornflakes, cocoa and coffee
Tim drinks tea and chews on his toffee

David reads dragon and dinosaur books
Harry is happy and fishes with hooks

Ivan's not well in fact he's quite ill
William's best friends just call him Will

Karl has a toy kangaroo and a kite
Nelly is naughty and stays up half the night.

Queenie likes birds and knows about quail
Sammy's new pet is a slow moving snail

Rosalind Roberts loves to race and to run
Freddie thinks flying is lots of fun

Ellie eats bacon and extra big eggs
Lily has very long arms and long legs


**Rhymes for names**

*These nonsense verses are silly rhymes rather than poems but children love them and they will help them to hear rhyming sounds from an early age. As they begin to understand this they will be able to help make up their own.*

Come on Fred
You sleepy head
It's time for bed
His mother said

Oh dear Will
You do look ill
Just take this pill
Said Auntie Lil (or Uncle Phil)

Cousin Lee
Climbed a tree
But hurt his knee
Oh dear me

Jennifer Mane
Ran down the lane
Run back again
Said Uncle Wayne

My friend Joe
Bumped his toe
He has to go
Really slow

My neighbour's cat
Which is very fat
Sat on her hat
And squashed it flat

My sister Jane
Loves the rain
Jumps in the puddles
Again and again

My baby Joe
Is very slow
Why can't he
Just get up and go?

## Shopping

(Phonics patterns and rhymes)

*The final verse includes '—-' to indicate that the reader should pause here to allow the children to complete the rhyme.*

I decided to go to the pet shop
I thought I'd buy a snake
But I ended up in the baker's
And so I bought a cake

I decided to go the baker's
Because I needed some bread
But I ended up in the butcher's
And bought some meat instead

I decided to go to the butcher's
To get sausages for tea
But ended up in the toy shop
And bought something just for me

I decided to go to the toy shop
I didn't know what to choose
So I went instead to the shoe shop
Because I needed new —— shoes

### Winter words

Slipping and sliding
Slowly gliding
on the ice
Slippety slop slippety slop
I can't stop I can't stop

### Thunder rhymes

*Ask the children to use some of these words to describe thunder and lightning, 'flash crash', 'rumble roll', 'jagged fork', before reading them the next poem.*

Thunder crashing
Lightning flashing
Rolling rumbling
Rain comes tumbling

### Rhyming verse

(written by Joshua age 4)

Would you like to eat a bug
Find a spider in your mug
Eat your jelly from a jug?

No thank you!
I would rather have a hug

## Reference

*Jasper's Beanstalk*, by Nick Butterworth and illustrated by Mick Inkpen 2008. Hodder Children's Books.

# Anthology index